on track ...
Lou Reed
1972-1986

every album, every song

Ethan Roy

T0243770

sonicbondpublishing.com

Sonicbond Publishing Limited
www.sonicbondpublishing.co.uk
Email: info@sonicbondpublishing.co.uk

First Published in the United Kingdom 2023
First Published in the United States 2023

British Library Cataloguing in Publication Data:
A Catalogue record for this book is available from the British Library

Copyright Ethan Roy 2023

ISBN 978-1-78952-283-9

Typeset in ITC Garamond Std & ITC Avant Garde Gothic
Printed and bound in England

Graphic design and typesetting: Full Moon Media

Follow us on social media:
Twitter: https://twitter.com/SonicbondP
Instagram: www.instagram.com/sonicbondpublishing_/
Facebook: www.facebook.com/SonicbondPublishing/

Linktree QR code:

This is my Lou Reed book.

Dedication

For Christian, whose own life was saved by rock 'n' roll when he realized how easy and fun it is to get his mother's goat by stomping about the house belting out 'Sally can't dance no more/ They found her in the trunk of a ford!'.

And in memory of Chris Gray.

Acknowledgements

Many thanks to Stephen Lambe at Sonic Bond Publishing for this truly life-changing opportunity, and great thanks and best love to my Elsie, who truly taught me the glory of love, which I can only hope to equally return, even though she continues to insist that 'Lou Reed looks like a Simpsons character!'

Special thanks to all my dear friends at O'Slattery's for keeping me well fed (and well drunk) during the composition of a large part of this book, as well as my good friends Colin and Lauren at Delaware Supply for precisely the same.

Author picture by Elise Alkurabi.

on track ...
Lou Reed

Contents

Introduction

To those in the know, Lou Reed is many things. He is the grandfather of this, the progenitor of that. He is the founder of X, he is the proto- of Y. He has been celebrated, denigrated, ignored, re-discovered, lionized, and eulogized, all several times in one lifetime. Even if you have read only this far, you most likely know exactly what I am talking about.

If Lou Reed had never recorded so much as another note after 23 August 1970, we would still have much to discuss; the brief, seminal history of The Velvet Underground deserves and duly receives weighty tomes of its own, a hundred times over. The purpose of this book is to explore and appreciate what came after when Lou Reed took his first tentative steps out of his parents' Freeport, Long Island home, where he had been resigned to self-exile, and once again began to honor his musical muse. Although some might find it apt to suggest that Lou's solo career really began with The Velvet Underground's third album in 1969, our work here begins in 1972 and extends to 1986. A second forthcoming volume picks up in 1989 and lasts to his final release in 2011. All of his solo albums will be considered, as well as major, album-length collaborations, and the live albums that he had a distinct hand in designing, producing, and realizing. At the end, there will be a brief appendix of additional recordings that offer glimpses and tastes of their own.

So, why Lou Reed? Well, for starters, there are the lyrics. Having received a B.A. with Honors from Syracuse University in Creative Writing in 1964, and studying under the troubling, radiant guidance of Delmore Schwartz, certainly places him amongst the refined literary canon, and while his work often reflects the various heights and depths of studied, belabored lines, he is primarily known for, and adept at scribing, some of the ugliest, grittiest, angriest, sexiest rock 'n' roll wordplay ever to be set to three (or fewer) chords. It is this duality in language that he is able to straddle so effortlessly and vigorously, song after song, album after album, that produces such vividness in his work. Moments of high and exalted celebration are often tethered to lamentations of vulgar and profound rage, filth, and alienation, typically within the same song. And then there are the points in between; mundanity, whimsicalness, and even triviality causing the listener to once again engage in the guesswork that each true Lou fan comes to expect and enjoy in their search for meaning and essence in the music. Lou does *not* hold back. He takes you there, every time. Sometimes the honesty, or the intensity of the honesty, can leave the listener almost cringing, unable to pay the fare. Other times, the listener is brought along to an interpersonal ceremony of sorts; a character or situational meditation that transcends the limitations of musical verse.

Then, there is the guitar. Lou Reed will never be included amongst the rapid-fire, all-fingers-of-both-hands, twice-the-speed-of-sound 'guitar heroes', and that is of no consequence. He exists in a sphere of one. From his earliest desires to make the guitar sound like the horn of Ornette Coleman or Archie Shepp, and then creating something wholly unique in and of itself, to his more refined, gear-oriented tonal shaping of the later years, Lou's axe work is his own. While he was never what could be called, either celebratorily or derisively, a *virtuoso*, the point is moot. His deeply personal and intensive approach to the instrument always suits the music's purpose in spades, not only in terms of actual notes played but also with regard to the intangible feel such an instrument is still capable of providing. Since his VU days, the guitar has occasionally been sidelined a bit in the place of Lou's role as singer, frontman, and bandleader, but the instrument, *his* instrument, is never far.

Your author's connection with Lou Reed is a bit of a puzzle, as it seems that Lou Reed has never *not* been there. I don't wish to suggest that my pre-pubescence was of the precocious sort that saw me studying and parsing the various character studies of abject misery that is *Berlin*, but as a child of the 1970s, growing up along the Hudson River, two hours and change north of New York City, Lou was there. 'Walk on the Wild Side' is deservedly still seen as an anthem of sorts for a number of reasons: the lyrics, the stories within the lyrics, the darker edges that slipped past the censors, the deadpan but deadly serious vocals, the dueling double and electric basses, that sax solo, and just the pure New York-ness of everything in the song. You do not have to set foot in any of the five boroughs to know that this sound *is* New York. It just feels right. One of the advantages of having intelligent and cultured divorced parents is that during any given school week, you might be informed that you will, in fact, not be going to school this coming Friday, as you and said parent will be boarding the train in Rensselaer, riding into (at the time) Grand Central, to begin the day at The Museum of Natural History to peruse dinosaur bones. This would then be followed by lunch at the Russian Tea Room, then onto a post-repast jaunt through Central Park, and concluding with a look at the Van Gogh exhibit at the Met, or even a Rousseau show at MOMA. To this out-of-town boy, the sights, sounds, smells, tastes, and feels of the place were inextricably captured in Lou's big hit like an ant in amber. Who knows why – it had to be that way.

A few years later, while hurtling towards the horns of adolescence, the video for 'Women' could actually be seen on early-days MTV. Perhaps once. The sparse presentation, with Lou in his omnipresent shades and black Telecaster, and the song itself, buoyed and propelled by Fernando Saunders' fretless bass, is low-key in the extreme. Yet, even to the initiate, it's Lou Reed. 'Hey, that's Lou Reed', said one of my two older brothers at the time. Moments later, after the second chorus, where Lou once again declares his amorous fealty, my one older brother chuckled, 'Yea, *right*!' to which my other older brother asked, 'Lou Reed is gay?' – '*Very*', confirmed the first. Despite our assumption being ambiguous at best, Lou's actual orientation was not a concern to any of us, nor did it color our impression of the artist in any way in the less-than-inclusive 1980s. We then began a spirited debate on the numerous musicians from the 1970s who found it not only fashionable but also lucrative to publicly declare some degree of 'sexual fluidity' in those heady times; standard conversation for budding music geeks.

At about the same time, Lou might appear on your TV hocking Honda motor scooters. This was the era when any still-surviving 'true believers' of rock 'n' roll could have their aged, decrepit illusions shattered anew by the spidery, ever-expanding relationship between 'truth' and 'business': some long-forgotten bread company hyping their wares to Canned Heat's version of 'Goin' Up the Country', The Ramones' near-sacred and sacrosanct 'Blitzkrieg Bop' asking us to participate in New York State's summer-long horse racing racket, or perhaps most egregious, Nike pedaling their shit to us to the tune of The Beatles' 'Revolution'. The Dream, if ever there actually was such a thing, was truly over.

With this fulsome baggage in mind, how bad was Lou's commercial? Set to the tune of (what else?) 'Walk on the Wild Side,' a busy camera pans through a fairly basic series of soft-focus nocturnal cityscapes: steam rising up from subway grates, headlights and taillights pouring through intersections, lovers, clasped in shadows, embracing. Near the end of the standard 30-second allotment, our man appears in black leather and shades, perched beside the featured product in question. With a Brando-esque swoop, he removes said shades and utters his five-word treatise on automotive commerce: 'Hey! Don't settle for wawkin'!' Truth be told, and as oxymoronic as this statement may seem, it's a cool commercial. Unlike most advertisements, it neither insults nor infantilizes the viewer, and its scenes and images are at the very least tasteful. As for Lou, he is Lou in the purest sense. There is no acting, posing, or contriving that would present something other than Lou in his few-second contribution, and to be sure, Lou did ride a bike, just not a Honda, and certainly not a scooter. As a commercial, it seems bizarrely real, and make no mistake, when it was on TV, viewers would momentarily pause and declare, 'Hey, that's Lou Reed'.

The aforementioned brief flickers – a song and its after-effects, a music video, and a TV commercial – were how Lou Reed was first presented to your author, and these impressions got the ball rolling weirdly, spectacularly. And this is before I even knew what a 'velvet underground' was.

Rock 'n' roll, even as we are knee-deep in the 21st century, can still be considered a language for the misfit, the alienated, the fuck-up, but only when our culture, as individual participants or *en masse*, is at its most expansive. Rock 'n' roll was first declared dead before its very birth was finalized, and the statements of impending mortality have never ceased. Trying to decide, once and for all, if rock 'n' roll is truly dead is about as futile as trying to decide, once and for all, what rock 'n' roll truly is. Just like Jenny, five years old, whose Life was saved by rock 'n' roll, it is a safe bet that Lou Reed could claim the same, as could your author, as could most likely anyone perusing this volume. Can this still happen? Is it still possible, in this day and age, to have a life saved by rock 'n' roll? Does it matter? Wheels within wheels, to say the least.

After 23 August 1970, Lou Reed had closed the door on a very distinct personal chapter, or series of chapters. What next? Serving as a typist in his father's accounting office was, by all accounts, a stopgap as Lou worked his way through what his various biographers have described as a post-VU nervous breakdown. With time and the support of both family and many friends, all offering their own distinct brew of reliability as well as being expendable, Lou Reed would again do what Lou Reed was meant to do, and he kept at it till his death.

Lou Reed (1972)

Personnel:
Lou Reed: vocals and guitar
Caleb Quaye: electric and acoustic guitars, piano
Steve Howe: electric guitar
Paul Keogh: electric and acoustic guitars
Rick Wakeman: piano
Les Hurdle: bass guitar
Brian Odgers: bass guitar
Clem Cattini: percussion
Kay Gardner: vocal harmonies
Helene Francis: vocal harmonies
Produced at: Morgan Studios, London, by Richard Robinson and Lou Reed
Engineer: Mike Bobak
Release date: US: 1 April 1972, UK: July 1972
Running time: 38:38
Highest chart places: US: 189, UK: did not chart

In his early post-VU days, Lou had been spending his leisure hours in the Manhattan apartment of Richard and Lisa Robinson, the husband-and-wife team of writers/producers/scenesters/tastemakers that were deeply enmeshed in the modes of the day. With Bettye Kronstad, his soon-to-be first wife at his side, Lou would frequently hold court at the Robinson's to a rapt audience of notables, peers, and admirers hanging on his every pronouncement and proclamation like word from on high. It must have been a salve to his bruised and battered ego, and it was Richard Robinson, along with record executive Dennis Katz, who were able to facilitate the release of Lou's still-standing contract to Atlantic Records and usher him onto the roster at RCA, Elvis' hometown, where Katz was employed. In grand style, Robinson and Reed decamped to London in order to cast off any vestigial connections, either musical or cultural, to NYC, and to also utilize what was understood to be the superior quality of London's recording studios and staff, with Robinson to serve as producer. In an even odder twist, many of the session musicians employed on the album, like Rick Wakeman and Steve Howe, were luminaries in the prog rock field; a genre as diametrically opposed to anything Lou Reed might be involved with as sonically possible. With all this in mind, what did Lou Reed serve up on his first solo outing? How might we describe this seminal offering?

In a word, lackluster. A cursory glance at the back sleeve shows us a picture of Lou on stage gesturing dramatically from a 1969 VU performance. The track list will ring many, many bells for anyone even remotely familiar with the man in question; eight out of the ten selections are revised and dusted-off VU chestnuts, long available on bootlegs, the rich and celebrated *Live 1969* VU album, and eventual legit-reissue 'bonus tracks'. This rehashing is a trend

13

that would continue at least throughout the first decade of his solo years – so much for distancing himself from the past.

It is the grand luxury of hindsight that provides the best view of *Lou Reed*. The informed listener knows that this, to borrow Lou's own line from much further down the road, is the beginning of a great adventure. The songs here are almost all familiar; the versions from over the years change arrangements and even lyrics as their creator continuously tinkers. The hard reality is that the versions of these songs are not the best they can be – as informed listeners, we know this. The proof is in the pudding. As for the album itself, there is little to commend it for. The production is flat, the playing competent but sparkless, and the singer tentative. The word 'tentative' is perhaps the most frequently used term to describe this album, and it fits. All things considered, this is not a bad album, but its greatest sin is just how totally and utterly ordinary it is. One wonders what Richard Robinson's role was in the studio in London at the beginning of 1972, and how it led to this final result. He and Lou would work together once more in 1978 for the fractious and charged sessions that would produce the brilliant *Street Hassle* LP. For now, we see Lou's first LP as a stepping stone for what's to come, and while it leaves much to be desired, we are all the better for it.

'I Can't Stand It' (Reed)
Blunka-Blunka drums count out four to lead us into this workman-like reading of this song. Two guitars play out their roles: one fuzzed in rhythm, one clean in melody. Lou barks out a good rock 'n' roll shout in the verses and is joined by Ms. Gardner and Ms. Francis in the chorus. Everything is pumping along in a perfectly functional way, but liftoff remains elusive. After a brisk two minutes and 38 seconds, we return to the idea of merely functional. With this particular song's many previous outings in mind, how does this version rate? It's not a patch off the top-of-the-heap version on 1985's *VU*, despite getting an E for effort, and there are some blistering live versions recorded live at La Cave, among other venues, but that was then, this is now.

'Going Down' (Reed)
The acoustic guitar and piano intro could very possibly place us in Asylum Records territory, but Lou's dry, slightly askew 'ballad-style' voice saves us from such a fate, despite being curiously buried in the mix. He sings as if he truly wants to believe in the lyric's tried-and-true tale of bleak realizations and deflated dreams, but he remains hesitant. This is an idea that runs roughshod throughout this album: *hesitancy*, as if the artist was just really not sure of what he was creating. This is especially clear on this 'new' song, heretofore unknown. The band, in their impeccable, professional way, keep things moving along, but the end results add up to precious little.

'Walk it and Talk It' (Reed)

Coming out of the gate with a decaffeinated Rolling Stones riff, this song quickly bares more muscle than any of the versions available as *Loaded*-era outtakes. Beyond that, it offers little else. An adequately skilled, busy guitar solo at two minutes and thirty seconds makes one yearn for Sterling Morrison, despite knowing better. Lou moves through his verses and choruses untroubled by conviction.

'Lisa Says' (Reed)

This track is hard to assess, as the *VU* version is just so, so superior. The saving grace here is that Lou retains the middle section – 'Why am I so shy...' – that we first hear on the *Live 1969* version. The swaggering, mid-tempo beat suggests the standard early 1970s post-country rock flavor, but the song remains there, mired in the most basic of stylistic representations.

'Berlin' (Reed)

Side one of the original LP concludes with seeds that would germinate and blossom into much heartier, juicer fruit in the future, but you wouldn't know that here, despite it being a truly new song at this outing. Rick Wakeman's cocktail piano sets the stage for our mini tableau of Lou's many lyrical images. Clem Cattini's soft brushwork compliments the mood as Lou reservedly croons about walls, height measurements, and syrupy liqueurs on ice. At 1:42, both guitars roll into a harmonious melodic exploration that lasts a bit and moves the musical proceedings along adequately. However, the listener can't help but pine for the song's penultimate representation a few years later, or at the very least, the unofficial live version recorded early in the year of this album's release at The Bataclan Club in Paris – featuring Lou, John Cale, and Nico – where Cale brightly and crisply handles said musical interlude on piano. The flat, cardboard-like sound that permeates the entire album does this track a distinct disservice, as Lou delivers a vocal performance that cautiously rises above the album's typically tepid delivery. The last 30 seconds of the song bring a pointless up-tempo vamp that suggests little more than a musical stage show's closing number. This final section was gladly dropped from the superior version of this song that caps the later album of the same name.

'I Love You' (Reed)

Side two starts off with 20 seconds of two gently picked acoustic guitars and smooth, slide-like melodic interjections from a clean electric. It would not be at all out of character to then hear the lulling vocal tones of, say, Roger McGuinn, Jim Croce, or even – God forbid – Brewer & Shipley, but Lou once again saves us from such a fate, if only barely. Gentle, bland folk-rock niceties float along for another two minutes while Lou pretends to give a shit about the by-the-number love lyrics that he sounds like he wishes he didn't have to sing.

'Wild Child' (Reed)

We get a bit of a reprieve from the over-arching banality that flows through the entire record with this track, which is not only sonically more than functional but almost fun as well. Lou's delivery raises its temperature noticeably, as he rolls through lyrics that blend his typical character-driven narrative with the occasional low-wattage, now-you-see-it, now-you-don't surrealism of his words that can both tickle and tempt the listener in equal measures. Various persons and their doings are listed and considered; in one set of verses, the soon-to-be Mrs. Reed #1 gets a mention with regard to the difficulties she faced as a young actor in the city, but all figures are at last united with the singer as their individual conferences consistently turn back to Lorraine, the song's true 'Wild Child'. Ultimately, it's just a nifty little rock 'n' roll song. At the conclusion of the second set of verses, just before the first chorus, Lou lets rip with a very uncharacteristic Jagger-esque yelp, as if to show the listener that he *really means* this one.

'Love Makes You Feel' (Reed)

This song, yet another polished-up relic from the near-past, stands out with regard to the fact that it is the album's most musically complex song. While that's not saying much, given the circumstances, it has far too many chords for a Lou Reed song. That's also about all it has. The lyrics, which revolve around the already generally settled idea that 'love makes you feel ten feet tall', are basic in the extreme; this simplicity is a literary effect that Lou has used to great, if not triumphant, effect over the years, but its strength is non-existent here. At two minutes and 20 seconds, Lou finishes yet another chorus with a spoken declaration of '...and it sounds like this', which leads the band into a tom-tom-driven rave-up with super-strummy guitars that lasts for 30 seconds before finding its denouement and returning the song to its original tempo and subsequent resolution. One imagines that this must have been one of Richard Robinson's suggestions that Lou actually heeded. This section does the song no service, but prog-rockers gonna' prog-rock.

'Ride Into the Sun' (Reed)

There are scores of *Loaded*-era outtakes of this song, usually, but not always, sung by Doug Yule, and they all trump this one, despite it being actually sung by Lou himself. This is a pity because done right, it's a great song. The sense of exhaustion and defeat that seems to soak the listener, while the singer tries to remind us that the city is 'just a flower made out of clay', is wholly absent here. The standard rock music arrangement begins with both guitars hacking away at a minor, three-chord descent, bringing to mind Bob Welch-era Fleetwood Mac, among other less-than-luminaries. As the song moves forward, both guitars pick up the steam with busy, note-drenched vamps and licks in tandem with each other while Lou snores through the verses.

'Ocean' (Reed)

Lou Reed's first solo LP ends with a long-favorite song for both himself and many listeners. Once again, the contemporary listener must adjust their expectations of this version to the many others in existence; the sparse, Moe Tucker-dominated take from *VU*, or the thundering, expansive live take from *Live 1969*, a personal favorite of Lou's, among others. By now, it probably does not need to be said, but this version is inferior, although not without its strengths due to the majesty of the song itself. The track both begins and ends with a solemn gong strike as if issuing both the commencement and completion of a ritual. A sense of atmosphere has always been a key ingredient to this song, and it is present here, with Lou finding his way up and down the peaks and crests of the lyrics that detail someone's struggle with sanity. He sounds just a bit more engaged here than on the lion's share of the album. At the start of the chorus section – 'Here come the waves/Down by the sea' – the piano, presumably played by Rick Wakeman, decoratively dances about the keys, suggesting incoming surf, while Clem Cattini rings out washes of ride cymbal to equal effect. At the close of each chorus, a guitar plays a four-note octave figure that stands out distinctly. At 3:42, the band halt, allowing for the three-chord anomaly that interrupts the established vibe. Lou brings us back into the song, singing 'Here come the waves', joined by Kay Gardner and Helene Francis, appropriately drenched in reverb. The climax builds with Lou's verse sung like an incantation, ever rising in intensity, until the wave crashes onto the shore and calmly recedes back out to where it came from, finally concluded by the closing gong strike. Despite being the truly weirdest song on Lou's first album, to either the benefit or detriment, or both, this one works.

Transformer (1972)

Personnel:

Lou Reed: lead vocals, rhythm guitar

Mick Ronson: lead guitar, piano, recorder, string arrangements

David Bowie: backing vocals, keyboards, acoustic guitar on 'Wagon Wheel', and 'Walk on the Wild Side'

Herbie Flowers: bass guitar, double bass, tuba on 'Goodnight Ladies' and 'Make Up'

John Halsey: drums

Trevor Bolder: trumpet

Ronnie Ross: soprano saxophone on 'Goodnight Ladies', baritone saxophone on 'Walk on the Wild Side'

Thunderthighs (Karen Friedman, Dari Lalou, and Casey Synge): backing vocals

Klaus Voorman: bass guitar on 'Perfect Day', 'Goodnight Ladies', 'Satellite of Love' and 'Make Up'

Barry DeSouza: drums

Ritchie Dharma: drums

Produced at Trident Studios, London, by David Bowie and Mick Ronson

Engineer: Ken Scott

Release date: 8 November 1972

Running Time: 36:40

Highest Chart Places: US: 29, UK: 13

Lou's first was a dud, both artistically and commercially – he was down, but not out. He still had some true believers out there, and some of them had a bit of clout to them. One of these folks happened to be David Bowie, who was still enthralled by the sounds provided to him on 'The Banana Album' from years previous. Bowie was one of the few who not only heard the album but was actually moved by its contents, and Bowie being Bowie, he never forgot a thrill. At the time, he was primed and ready for world takeover with his impending *The Rise and Fall of Ziggy Stardust and the Spiders From Mars* release. While not yet blessed with a bona fide international hit, his previous albums moved from strength to strength, and with the taste of global domination on his palette, he did what any enterprising entertainer would do: he bought up the competition.

This take is cynical in the extreme, but it's a fun idea to bandy about. Bowie first booted Mott The Hoople out of a four-album rut with his gift of 'All The Young Dudes', allowing a brilliant band to finally have their brilliance recognized, both culturally and financially. Lou was next, and *Transformer* would be the combination of an artistic and commercial watershed of sorts that had eluded Lou before, and would, alas, continue after, his connection with Bowie. They would remain friends for the duration of their lives, but as with all relationships with Lou, it would run the gamut of warm to frosty and back again, with accusations and recriminations aplenty. At Trident Studios, however, the mood was up and energized. While Bowie receives primary credit as the producer, it was his secret weapon wunderkind guitar player Mick Ronson truly running the engine room. This is not to say that Bowie was another there-in-name-only eminence grise like Andy Warhol during the production of the first VU album; his aural presence, not to mention his actual voice, runs throughout the LP, but Ronson chopped wood and carried water diligently, and the finished product is as much his as Bowie's with regard to production. Not only was his distinct guitar pivotal to the songs, with its slippery yet uncharacteristically restrained licks and cocked wah pedal tonal experiments, but his string arrangements move certain tracks from good to great. His presence here cannot be underestimated.

This is also the album where Lou began to work with image. While the purpose of this book is to focus on the music, the process that Lou embarked upon – indeed, a *transformation* – started here and would continue to morph and permutate throughout his career. We would see him go from cosmeticized 'Glam Phantom' to ambisexual, tight leather speed lizard, to scotch-soaked, bloated balladeer, to stern, sober, settled married man, to disgruntled socio-political discontent, to avant-garde NYC grandpappy of Arts and Letters. Have I missed anything? Most likely, but we cannot deny the important role that persona played to Lou Reed, something he both relished and reviled, and it began with this album.

After this, Bowie would attempt a trifecta with Iggy and the Stooges with checkered results, but Lou was off and running on a debauched ten-year ride that would see him playing the stages of the world, moving from one tempestuous personal relationship to the next, releasing music that perambulated from the sacred to the profane, often simultaneously, rattling and raging against a scrolling cast of real and perceived foes and/or friends, and consuming a fuck-ton of drugs. In short, Lou Reed was now a rock 'n' roll star.

The completion of this album and its subsequent success seemed to speak to a long promise at last fulfilled. After roughly ten years of struggle, from college beer bands to trend-chasing hack work at Pickwick Records, to arty obscurity, to collapse, to tentative rejuvenation and fragile first attempts, *Transformer* is where the dividends finally began to be paid. Lou Reed had, with a bit of help, finally done it his way. He was singing about what he wanted to sing about in front of a rock 'n' roll band without compromising his vision or muse and he even earned a hit to show for it. After all these years and tears, success was finally his. He could now continue, on his own terms, to ride the waves of musical and artistic success. Now that the keys were his, how hard could it be to just keep turning the locks? If only!

'Vicious' (Reed)

The LP locks into its first groove with a cowbell-dominated stomp wed to thudding bass and two hard-working guitars. As soon as Lou opens his mouth, it is clear that his level of commitment to the proceedings is higher

than anything from his previous LP, and it would remain so throughout
each selection on this new offering. What started as an offhand suggestion
about a new song from Andy Warhol, suggesting that someone hit someone
else with a flower, has been turned into a full-chested declaration of intent.
After each chorus, Ronson elevates things with a busy, scratchy attack at the
guitar strings. Its balanced position in the mix serves it with just the right
combination of boldness and restraint that prevents it from spilling over into
yet another big guitar event that had been littering music everywhere for the
past few years and would continue to do so for the next few decades. Bowie
first makes his presence known on the album with the ghostly voices that
conclude each chorus, and by the second time around, the song's tempo has
noticeably quickened, indicating that the boys in the band were feeling it.
Why don't *you* swallow razor blades?

'Andy's Chest' (Reed)

The first of two reshaped songs from the past (the other being 'Satellite of
Love') has been given a drastic overhaul from the bouncy, peppy version first
cut by the VU. Lou has occasionally suggested that this song is a love letter
of sorts, describing how he felt about Andy Warhol being shot by radical
feminist artist Valerie Solanas in 1968. This moody reading starts with a
whisper and a strummed guitar, while Lou states his druthers to be a bat if
given a choice to become anything that is capable of flight. At 53 seconds
in, the drums cough out the fattest, pudding-est fill to bring the song to its
proper place. It is here that Bowie once again adds his harmonized chorus in
a reverb sea. This is one of Lou's great songs where the lyrics have a life of
their own, unmarried to the music. Passages like 'Oh, all the trees are calling
after you/And all the venom snipers after you/Are all the mountains bolder
after you?' among others, can take on many different lives of their own when
presented spoken, or read directly from the text. This is only the beginning.

'Perfect Day' (Reed)

Lou's big ballad. While 'Walk on the Wild Side' is undoubtedly the career-
cementing breakout hit from the album, this track has slow-burned its way to
a legacy all its own. This soft, delicate lover's meditation on a perfect lover's
afternoon has not only been repeatedly used for various sundry products and
placements but has also suffered its fair share of misinterpretation over the
years. The song begins with a weightless piano and percussion duet that is
soon joined by Lou's pin-drop vocals. By the second set of verses, the listener
is then gifted with the introduction of Mick Ronson's truly heavenly string
score – the glistening backbone of the whole piece. A grand crescendo is
achieved at the chorus with swirling strings and Lou's double-tracked vocals,
not so much sung as emanated from some lofty peak.

Perhaps the greatest appeal is the hovering darkness that the lyrics show
to be just beneath the surface of a song of clear romantic devotion. The

shadows cast themselves long and looming in the song's final three verses: 'Just a perfect day, you made me forget myself/I thought I was someone else, someone good', and then even more cryptically, the song ends with 'You're going to reap just what you sow'. To a public that likes its expressions of love to be all about love and nothing but, all the time, these closing remarks can raise eyebrows. What is going on here? One interpretation that gained traction but was summarily dismissed by both author and muse was the idea that the song detailed fond moments between two drug addicts; this was bolstered by the song's inclusion in Danny Boyle's 'Hey kids! Junkies are NEAT!' 1996 film *Trainspotting*. Both Lou and ex-wife Bettye Kronstad, for whom the song was composed, have gone on record saying such an idea is, plainly, tosh, but some remain unconvinced.

25 years after the LP's release, this song was given a revitalization when the BBC trotted out a star-studded remake of the song for an oddly self-promotional video meant to highlight the BBC's long-standing commitment to musical and cultural diversity. The version featured a solid representation of still-up-and-taking-nourishment legends (Elton John, Bono, David Bowie, Shane McGowan, Tammy Wynette, and of course, Lou himself, et al) as well as a sprinkling of 1997's contemporary glitterers (Huey Morgan, Skye Edwards, Evan Dando, Heather Small, Boyzone, et al). After much public demand, the song was officially released in November of that year as a Children in Need charity single, where it not only went to the number one singles position in the UK, Ireland, Scotland, and Norway but also did remarkably well throughout continental Europe. Perfect Day, indeed.

'Hangin' Round' (Reed)

One of *Transformer*'s 'deep cuts', to be sure, but a rocking good time at that. Lou's voice jumps out of the box at once, spinning another one of his set of tales about various characters and their various characterizations: Harry – a rich young man, Jeanie – a spoiled young brat, Kathy – a bit surreal. What these human oddities have to do with one another is not disclosed, nor does it need to be. Their troublesome, eccentric doings all revolve around and settle back to the chorus: 'You keep hangin' 'round me/and I'm not so glad you found me/You're still doin' things that I gave up years ago'. The wordplay is as colorful and vivid as only Lou can do in one of his expansive character studies: 'Harry was a rich young man, who would become a priest/ He dug up his dear father, who was recently deceased' along with 'Hark the herald angels sang and reached out for a phone/And plucking it with a knife in hand dialed long distance home'. Musically, the bass guitar is welded to the bass drum and it brings the bounce, while Ronson's riffs boost from the sidelines. The icing on the cake is at the chorus, where the piano plays simple eights that solidify the song's rock 'n' roll guts. A great bubbly breakup song, for those in the market for such a thing.

'Walk on the Wild Side' (Reed)

The one for the vaults and ages. It is often seen in pop culture that a certain artist's 'big hits' are typically pale detractions from the artist's greater oeuvre on account of the various and multi-limbed commercial considerations and alterations that must often go into the creation and promotion of said 'hit' material. This song, Lou's 'biggest' before or since, misses that rubric. Without even addressing the lyrics, this is one of the weirdest sounding 'big hits' in pop culture. It lacks all of the essential cornerstone components of a hit: the bigness and the brightness; short and quick returns, both musical and lyrical; the streamlined simplicity. This is by no means the only hit pop outlier to come along; that is a genre in and of itself, but this one is just so, so good.

Herbie Flowers dominates the song with his double bass/electric bass counterpoint that is nothing less than a shining revelation to the very role of that instrument in music, and everyone else falls in. Brushed drums provide a loping, walking rhythm that allows Lou to begin one of his greatest character examinations: Holly Woodlawn, from Miami, FLA; Candy Darling, from out on the island; 'Little' Joe Dallesandro, who never once gave it away; the elusive Sugar Plum Fairy, Warhol film actor Joe Campbell, who came and hit the streets; Little Jacky Curtis, just speeding away. They are all individuals, with their own lives, all on the wild side. What do they share? How do they differ? Please re-read the previous declaration. These are the kinds of people Lou sought time and time again to bring into song. Have characters like these been celebrated in such a way before, or since? Yes, of course, but not pouring out from radios everywhere in the spring of 1973. Drug use, transvestitism, sucking cock – this was not 'pop hit' material. And yet here it is, as cool and serious as a funereal slab.

This song, along with the front and back cover images on this album, served as a lifeline to many far-removed, faceless, friendless, scattered persons, perhaps struggling to come to terms with messages they might have been receiving from themselves, concerning ideas of gender, sexual orientation, love, togetherness, identity. In places where any concept of fluidity of the aforementioned ideas might not have been welcomed, if not outright forbidden, a sense of possibility, of actually *belonging*, was unflinchingly proposed and vividly celebrated here. This song acknowledged feeling different, wanting to be different, having no choice *but* to be different, and somehow knowing or at least wishing to know what to do with these ideas and feelings; Lou recognized you and wanted you to know that it just might be ok, because he knew, too. What a tremendous message, a message that has never, nor will ever, lose its potency or necessity for all persons, everywhere.

And it only adds fuel to the fire, being that the music itself is just so killer. The aforementioned bass and drums pushing things along so gently yet strongly, Lou's easy, smooth, no-hassle delivery, Ronnie Ross' vocal and verbal bari sax solo that perfectly encapsulates a checkered cab's pointed, herky-jerky progress from Washington Heights to The Battery, with pertinent stops in between. Mick Ronson treats us to another cloaked, ethereal string arrangement that seems to hover at one thoroughly crucial unified note, only to sneakily move into subtle and restrained harmonies that never upstage anything. And then there are the 'colored girls': Karen Friedman, Dari Lalou, and Casey Synge, AKA Thunderthighs. Rising up from a sidewalk grate or subway entrance, their 'Doot-de-Doos' truly make the song. Hovering in like urban pre-dawn dew, they fade just as briskly as a car horn, a door slam, a thrown bolt – pure New York, pure Lou Reed. Four minutes and sixteen seconds of pure musical everything.

As legend has it, the song was originally commissioned from Lou for a planned stage production of Nelson Algren's 1956 novel, *A Walk on the Wild Side*, and the show's producers felt that Lou was the best songwriter (after Ray Davies, as Lou would remark onstage years later) available to capture their characters' gritty realities. The project was soon dropped when the producers were given the opportunity to stage *Mahogany*, which would go on to spawn a hit film and a hit theme song all its own. Lou, ever the frugal craftsman, kept his song, inhabited it with his own real-life characters, and birthed an anthem.

'Make Up' (Reed)

A bobbing, two-note bass figure starts the proceedings, and the singer shares the fond, dreamy sentiment of 'Your face when sleeping is sublime', which is then followed by a crisp run of notes on a tuba. Both the bass and tuba are owned and operated by Herbie Flowers, who runs the track, and the voice belongs to you-know-who. What first floats along as a lover's gentle teasing of their swain's cosmetic routine is shifted slightly when the chorus announces: 'Now we're coming out/Out of our closets/Out on the streets/Yeah we're coming out'. In 1973, the term 'coming out', while being known somewhat esoterically by those to whom it might apply, did not have the broad social understanding as a term for freely living and acknowledging one's gender, orientation, and identity that it does in contemporary times. Originally, the idea of 'coming out of the closet' as it relates to LGBTQ persons is thought to have originated from the early 20th century, where a person's entry into gay/lesbian subculture was seen as akin to the coming out of a debutante in the presentation of her newfound marriageable status among upper-class society. The first National Coming Out Day was later established on 11 October 1988 by Robert Eichberg, William Gamble, and Jean O'Leary. In 1973, just like with the previous song, to hear these things being mentioned and encouraged in pop music could be seen as a beacon of hope and possibility beyond whatever bleak, limiting surroundings and lack of possibilities someone might face in their pursuit to live a freer, more open life.

'Satellite of Love' (Reed)

Our second revived VU chestnut gives us a brisk, breezy, infinitely hummable tune that obscures what the lyrics disclose as the singer's gripping paranoia, to the point of obsession, about a wandering lover. Is the satellite in question an actual surveillance device, employed to root out a partner's unfaithfulness? The striding piano chords that anchor the song, both in their physical manifestation as well as the melodic steps they take, move about in such a way as to actually suggest physical levitation; of a satellite, a person, or the hopes and fears of a worried soul. The kicker is Bowie's baying hound backing vocals, with his coy 'Bom-Bom-Bom' in the chorus, to his upper-register soaring at the song's extended fade out – he truly performs valid service to the song and its singer.

'Wagon Wheel' (Reed)

This track seems to be a bit of a collage of three separate, half-completed songs. The first section, the basic rock 'n' roll core of the song, begins with Lou asking for someone to be his wagon wheel. He is then, curiously, answered by the Thunderthighs trio with a chirping 'Spoke! Spoke!' after the first verse. This quirky vocal interjection was apparently their idea. The groove treads along, with Lou's verbal encouragement to enjoy oneself, alongside the added thought of: 'But iffn' you think that you get kicks from flirting with danger/Just kick her in the head and rearrange her'. Then, at almost one minute in, the second section kicks in; a weirdly ambient passage that sees Lou go Catholic:

Oh heavenly father what can I do
What she's done to me is making me crazy
Oh heavenly father I know I have sinned
But look where I've been
It's making me lazy

Is this a reckoning with the past, just lazy wordplay, or both? After this, we see a return to the first verse again, and things round off with the third and final section, the 'Wake Me/Shake Me' part, where Lou is joined by Thunderthighs to the fade-out. This is the LP's title that can be said most closely abuts the 'filler' category.

'New York Telephone Conversation' (Reed)

One-and-a-half minutes of high parody; catty, campy, urbanite snark paying tribute to itself, and having a ball doing so. Apparently cut live in the studio, it features drums, bass, Bowie on piano and harmony, and Lou on vocals. Not taking too seriously a glittering social subsect that takes itself much too seriously, Lou sends up NYC friends and acquaintances that he is no doubt loathe to be a part of, yet even more loathe to do without, and Bowie cannot help but to play along heartily – after all, he would know, too. The music prances about like a stage audition, never once upstaging the performers in the spotlight.

'I'm So Free' (Reed)

The most Bowie-esque track of the bunch. From the full-throttle opening crunch, the listener can be forgiven should they think their ears are being occupied by Messrs. Ronson, Bolder, and Woodmansey, but it is not the case. This uncomplicated song keeps the rubber on the road throughout, while Lou sings about not much, it seems. The era-popular idea of 'Mother Nature's Son' is self-applied to the vocalist, which is just a bit out of character for our Lou and his justifiable disdain for all things 'hippy'. Mick Ronson squeezes off some truly tasty wah-wah licks in the right channel, but just as with his work on 'Vicious', they never hog the mic, as the proceedings roll to the fade.

'Goodnight Ladies' (Reed)

The perfect closing track at just the right speed and flavor. The wobbly, half-cocked, sun-is-almost-up dance band tempo serves the song's, and the album's, 'end of the show' vibe perfectly. Tuba and soprano sax flavor the clockwork rhythm respectfully, while Lou sings a lament for a departed love. The bridge:

> Now if I was an actor or a dancer who was glamorous
> Then you know an amorous life would soon be mine
> But now the tinsel light of starbreak
> Is all that's left to applaud my heartbreak
> And at 11 o'clock I watch the network news

The party's over, the booze is all gone; what the hell you still doin' here? 'Anyway, my TV dinner's almost done/It's a lonely Saturday night'. Fade to black and roll credits.

Acoustic demos of 'Hangin' Round' and 'Perfect Day' have appeared as bonus tracks on some issues. They feature Lou and his acoustic hacking away, with some interesting but by no means essential early drafts of lyrics that did not make the final cut, although it must be mentioned that the opening strums of 'Perfect Day' feature what would become the main melody of 'Ennui' from *Sally Can't Dance* a few years later in the root note of each chord. Lou sings and strums in fine form, but little is added to the overall grandeur that these songs would become.

Berlin (1973)

'The Company':
Michael Brecker: tenor sax
Randy Brecker: trumpet
Jack Bruce: bass (except 'Lady Day' and 'The Kids')
Aynsley Dunbar: drums (except 'Lady Day' and 'The Kids')
Bob Ezrin: piano and mellotron
Steve Hunter: electric guitar
Tony Levin: bass on 'The Kids'
Allan Macmillan: piano on 'Berlin'
Gene Martynec: acoustic guitar, synthesizer, and vocal arranging on 'The Bed',
bass on 'Lady Day'
Jon Pierson: bass trombone
Lou Reed: vocals and acoustic guitar
Dick Wagner: background vocals and electric guitar
Blue Weaver: piano on 'Men of Good Fortune'
B.J. Wilson: drums on 'Lady Day' and 'The Kids'
Steve Winwood: organ and harmonium
'The Choir': Bob Ezrin, Dennis Ferrante, Steve Hyden, Elizabeth March, Lou
Reed, Dick Wagner
Produced by: Bob Ezrin
Engineer: Jim Reeves
Arrangement: Allan Macmillan
Basic Tracks: Morgan Studios, London, recorded by Robin Black and Peter
Flanagan
Overdubbing: CTS Studios, London, by Richard Lewzey, and The Record Plant,
New York, by Greg Calby, Dennis Ferrante, Jim Frank, Joe Lopes, Pat Martin, Jay
Messina, Jim Reeves, Ed
Sprigg, Danny Tuberville, and Shelly Yakus
Mixed: The Record Plant, New York
Release date: 5 October 1973
Running time: 49:26
Highest chart places: US: 98, UK: 7

It's 1973: the dues have been paid and the coin is rolling in – it's time for
the grand artistic statement. Many, many recording artists would cross that
line, especially in the late-1960s and continuing unabated in the 1970s,
with spectrum-like results. Oftentimes these 'expressions' were double-LP
megaliths, but even when the proceedings had been reduced to a single
record, the content within was no less dramatic. Some were instant hits,
finding a place and position with the public that suggests a message just
waiting to be received. Others fell flat and hit hard, before even leaving the
ground, fettered and submerged by their lofty pretensions, bait-and-switch
unfulfilled promises, or just basic musical and conceptual ineptitude. Then

there are those that fell through the cracks, only to be reassessed and revived by time and tide. I'm sure you can tell where this is going.

Lou Reed poured everything he had into the making of *Berlin*; not only everything he had, but everything his wife had, everything producer Bob Ezrin had, and most likely everything the star-studded supporting musicians and studio technicians had as well. Judging from the sheer surplus of players, engineers, and actual studios involved in the realization of this artistic vision, it was a test of endurance for all at hand. At its conclusion, Lou's marriage to Bettye Kronstad would be in shambles, producer Bob Ezrin would be in rehab, and Lou's own drink and drug intake would be well on their way to the towering heights that are considered to be a rugged component of his myth and legend, let alone actual reality.

As for the album itself, it stands independently, not only among Lou's canon but among rock music's magnum opuses as a whole. For the initial tracks, he returned to London's Morgan Studios, where he cut his first solo LP, with a producer who was quickly rising in the ranks as the next man with the big sound. Bob Ezrin had already made his bones by dragging Alice Cooper (the band) into the spotlight; after *Berlin*, he would give KISS their long-delayed studio success with *Destroyer* and finish the decade helming Pink Floyd's excessive statement on rock star excess, *The Wall*. His sonic and technical expertise were matched only by his innate and ebullient enthusiasm, which would seem like the perfect yin to our Lou's sometimes surly, recalcitrant yang. It would seem.

The story that centers and accentuates *Berlin* is sordid in the extreme. A couple, Jim and Caroline, thoroughly in love with one another, fall victim to suspicion, drug abuse, infidelity, hatred, violence, and ultimately, suicide. Lou examines and illuminates these characters' misery and suffering with layered, multi-hued aplomb, as only he can. Despicable deeds and horrifying emotions are wrought large and real with no feeble requests for patience or sympathy, as none would or could be given, or so it might be suggested. Lou's desire to plumb the depths of humanity's shadows and shames is one of his greatest strengths as a writer, singer, and artist. From whence does such a black tide spring?

By 1973, the 'singer-songwriter' trope was in full effect, presented as the post-1960s 'next big thing' in pop music. James Taylor graced the cover of *Newsweek Magazine* in 1971, and following dutifully along thereafter, gentle persons with gentle acoustic guitars were being offered up as a more sensible option for a 'youth culture' that was now approaching, if not already entrenched within, their 30s. They were most likely ready to put away their previous youthful activities and frivolous concerns, like 'protest' and 'psychedelia'. As a result, emanating from radios everywhere, thin, pallid voices would meekly indicate to their listeners some key concerns: in case you were curious, the son of an esteemed horror movie actor would let you know that he's 'Easy', or another singer might sheepishly whine about how 'It don' matter to me', or, Heaven forfend, you might be regaled with details about a southbound journey on the back of an unnamed equine. As with anything, this 'new' singer-songwriter guise was hardly new at all; it reached back clearly and squarely to the previous decade's early interest in folk music, and it relished that music's outwardly suggested concepts of artistic and emotional integrity and legitimacy. Gone were the pursuits of hype, image, guile, or commerce. What existed in the place of those crass concepts was just the singer, their acoustic instrument, and a song composed by said performer that came from a place deeply within themself: truth, honesty, and above all, a sense of autobiography. This singer, perhaps even this 'star', was singing to you about themself, and the listener was being allowed to softly enter and relate.

Alas, like all things with any kind of a price tag or 'for sale' label affixed to it, this too, was pure bullshit, but for a while, it worked. If someone was singing a song to you, you were learning truthful things that the singer knew, perhaps even lived. Lou Reed always made it known that he wanted to be more than just a rock 'n' roll star; his literary ambitions were always placed at the forefront of the many faces and masks he would don throughout his career. So, with the tenor of the times being what it was for 1973, how much of *Berlin* is autobiographical, and how much is literary construction? This question would be the very hellhound barking at Lou's heels for his entire life, and it would be applied consistently to his entire catalog. At times, Lou delighted in the ambiguity, describing himself as merely a songwriter, who like any writer, must create characters and situations from either whole cloth, or a vast and seasoned blend of the real, the proto-real, and the fictional. At other times, some of Lou's songs seemed too hard and too harsh, in both their anger and their directness, to be anything but borne from personal experience. Yet he would bristle and snap at any probing of a song's non-fictional accuracy, all the while repeatedly insisting that all of his characters and situations were as real as the TV news. There are many, many of his songs that are either directly concerned with, or at the very least a reference to, his family, particularly his father, his youth, his erratic mental health, his relationships, and his excesses. Many would be held up to strong white light by critics, fans, or actual family members and intimates in an attempt to suss out the fact from the fiction. These are of course perfectly valid questions for any audience of any artist, not to mention most certainly serving as raw red meat to music geeks far and wide. If any kind of definitive answers or results can be divined, they must ultimately be subjected to the mercurial whims and caprices of the listener, the critic, the archivist, the interviewer, along with the artist themself. Lou has often gone on record declaring the profound and unstinting influence of Andy Warhol, an artist who trafficked, if not outright reveled in, whims and caprices, among other slippery and suggestively self-serving approaches to 'the truth'.

How much of *Berlin* Lou Reed and his wife Bettye Kronstad actually did or did not 'live', or how 'truthful' of a narrator the singer is, is of no consequence. The album remains the foreboding, darkly glittering gem it always has been. Reviled at its release in Lou's country of origin, but doing rather well in the UK, this 'Sergeant Pepper of the 70s', as the atrocious ad hype declared at the time, has been reconsidered and revalued in the decades following its birth. It would not be the first nor the last time such a thing would happen to something involving Lou Reed.

Lou was deeply devastated by the commercial failure and critical coolness of *Berlin*; as previously mentioned, it barely charted in the US, and this was in the afterglow of 'Walk on the Wild Side'. As we will see, Lou would revisit *Berlin* in grand style many years later, but at the time, the sting of failure was poisonous. This experience cost Lou a great deal personally, professionally, and chemically, among other fees, and he would continue to pay long after this album was in the rear-view mirror. So, he did what any rock 'n' roll star would do: he put a kick-ass band together and got back on the road.

'Berlin' (Reed)
Firing off with a howling, unsettling, possibly inebriated M.C. leading us through some half-cocked nightclub birthday celebration, this fades into a colorful flourishment on piano played by Andy Macmillan, introducing us to the song's chords and melody. After the tune makes its presence known, the singer enters after the briefest of pauses. Lou barely registers above a gasp as he revisits a previous exercise. The comparisons stop dead at this juncture; Lou's emotional commitment to his vocals, while hushed and subdued, is stunning, and the full sonic palette on offer here, courtesy of Bob Ezrin, has a lush and panoramic dimension to it heretofore absent from any previous recording with Lou Reed on it. Both of these key components are established within seconds of listening, and they would remain for the LP's duration. The previous version's bridge section – 'You're Right and I'm Wrong' – as well as some of the more capricious verses, such as 'Don't forget/Hire a vet...' have been left aside, and the song is better for it. This more than adequately sets the stage for all to come.

'Lady Day' (Reed)
Three quick strikes and the band arrive. This song, ostensibly an ode to Billie Holliday, the original 'Lady Day', seems out of place among the components of the story behind the album, but that's no matter. Kept aloft by Steve Winwood's lurking Hammond organ chords, the listener is told of a woman who passed by a bar and '...had to go in and sing/It had to be that way'. After the conclusion of the woman's song, she is seen returning to the hotel 'that she called home/It had greenish walls/A bathroom in the hall'. Is this the true Lady Day of jazz legend herself, or is this Caroline, without Jim, reveling in a moment of risky liberation only to return to the now changing and

suppressive mundanity of their union? Only the singer knows for sure. The track's musical arrangement stands out for its complexity in odd ways; during the chorus section, the tempo stutters and slows just a barely perceptible degree. Such a minor alteration not only requires instrumental competency of the highest order but the effect it creates within the music cannot be missed by any pair of ears due to its subtle but jarring result.

'Men of Good Fortune' (Reed)

This study of paternal dichotomy starts with tinkling piano and rhythm guitar thoroughly soaked in era-appropriate phase shifter, while Jack Bruce first makes his presence known on the LP with uncharacteristically restrained, yet still melodically busy and tonally fuzzy bass guitar. As with the previous track, this song's place within the narrative of Jim and Caroline is unclear: is Jim painfully studying his own origin with spiteful regret, or is this song much closer to home for its author? A great deal of Lou's lyrics, as well as his personal history, or at least as much as he has made available to disclose, has centered around the concept of the 'father wound'; the inevitable friction and emotional upheaval that will, some say must, occur between father and son. Resentment and disappointment, on both generational sides, loom large throughout his literary canon. Here, the 'rich son wait(ing) for his father to die' is offset by his counterpart in much less fortunate circumstances: 'The poor just drink and cry'. These comparisons are lined up and listed as the song moves from one set of verses to the next, but there are some surprises. Not all is so rosy for the men of good fortune: 'Men of good fortune/Very often can't do a thing/While men of poor beginnings/often, can do anything'. This suggests a certain bleak liberation for a man who is not indebted to his filial legacy. He cannot depend on his family's 'old money' because no such thing exists for him. As a result, his future, destitute as it may seem, presents certain options forbidden and unavailable to the rich young man, who despite the endless possibilities that his money supposedly guarantees, ultimately must follow his family's instructions and fulfill his family's expectations of a young, upstanding man that is worthy of his family's largesse. A man of good fortune can, of course, break his gilded bondage to his father by steadfastly embarking on a life path of his own design, but this typically results in disappointment, regret, or even outright banishment. This, too, is an idea frequently revisited by Lou: a father's or whole family's disappointment in their son, and the heavy toll this takes. Yet, in most characteristic fashion, Lou concludes each set of verses with an unmistakably blasé summation of the whole thing: 'But me, I just don't care at all'.

'Caroline Says I' (Reed)

Four songs in, Lou adds some real muscle to his vocals, and this track, the first of the two 'Carolines', follows accordingly. Since 1968, Lou had a list of women who 'said' in his songs: Stephanie, Candy, Lisa, and now Caroline.

It's a neat literary trick that allows the singer or narrator to respond to another character's impressions with their own first-person ideas. Here, Jim is lamenting Caroline's many barbed tongue skewerings of his masculinity. 'Caroline says that I'm just a toy/She wants a man, not just a boy' is about as clear and direct as can be. Jim takes her lashings and bristles under their sting, but he is not surprised to be subject to them: 'Just like poison in a vial, Hey, she was often very vile/But of course, I thought I could take it all'. Despite knowing that such a fire lurked within his love, he believed that these storms could be duly weathered. Now, he is not so sure, but he will not throw in the towel: 'She says she doesn't want a man who leans/ Still she is my Germanic queen'. The orchestral flourishes and choral clouds that uplift and round out the song to its conclusion add to its emotional fiber accordingly.

'How Do You Think it Feels' (Reed)

The album's only true rock 'n' roll song, and it's a greasy one. Bass and piano welcome us to the melody for a few bars, and they are then joined by Aynsley Dunbar's rumbling tom-tom and double bass drum thunder that ups the dramatic quotient just enough for Lou to step right in and attend to business. And what business it is: a seedy, slimy speed freak's lament on all things speed freak. 'How do you think it feels/And when do you think it stops!' could be seen as a statement on any variety of pain, physical or mental, but here it is undeniably specific. 'If only I had a little/If only I had some change/ If only, if only, only' is just the beginning of the list of coming-down woes the singer faces. Once again, the listener must ask, is this Jim? Is this Lou? Is this both of them in collage? It is a song that most definitely speaks to first-hand experience, with Lou erratically grunting/pleading someone to 'C'mere, Baby'/'Get down here, Mama' at the end of key lines.

If this wasn't enough, Steve Hunter at 1:24 thoroughly erases any doubt of legitimacy. He has already been flirting with the song; he enters at the beginning along with Lou, and he offers a choice liquid statement at the close of the first set of verses, but this is the actual guitar solo, and it is a fucking crusher. Each bend, each squeeze, each vibrato is a vast vocabulary unto themselves. With this lead, he simultaneously honors the vocal melody while also saying something completely unique and vital at the same time, deeply submerged in the rich tonal affirmations afforded by a Les Paul and analog phasing. Little wonder that Lou plucked him, along with compatriot Dick Wagner, to be central figures in his touring band for the next year. This dual guitar combination would, as we will soon see, distinguish itself as a significant chapter to the Lou Reed legacy. As the song chugs along, we are treated to fat, balls-out bursts of horns that add a vitamin jolt of Stax/Volt urgency to the foundation. 'How do you think it feels/When you've been up for five days/ Hunting around always/'Cause you're afraid of sleeping' is about as soiled and desperate as you can get, and that is what this song is a celebration of.

'Oh, Jim' (Reed)

This song, the last on side one of the LP, is where the album's narrative really begins to gel and coalesce. Like the title track, as well as the cinematic grand finale, 'Sad Song', this song reaches back to the past, but only just barely. This song was originally birthed as 'Oh Gin' in the summer of 1970 during the *Loaded* sessions in barely finished demo form. There is little in that primordial take to distinguish itself, and the only thing shared with this, the penultimate version, is the desperate interrogation the singer makes as to how they could 'be treated this way', but there is much territory to cover before that. This is a song in two distinct sections. The first gently fades in with a drum-and-bass tumble as the last strains of the previous track die away. They rise to a dominant volume, joined, perhaps, by a sweltering synthesizer drone, and then Lou jumps in. He's got a lot to say here, and once again, what he says blurs the line between fact and fiction, perhaps to the strongest degree of all the songs on this album:

All your two-bit friends they're shootin' you up with pills
They said that it was good for you, that it would cure your ills

and

All your two-bit friends, they asked you for your autograph
They put you on the stage, they thought it'd be good for a laugh

Seeming pretty close to the bone, they appear to share little with what we know of the character Jim. Both sections of verses are wrapped up quite cruelly and succinctly with 'And when you're filled up to here with hate... Beat her black and blue and get it straight', and then, most caustically, 'But I don't care just where it's at/'Cause honey I'm just like an alley cat'. 'Not caring' is a key theme throughout this whole story; no matter how ugly the deed, no matter how desperate the circumstance, ultimately, the voice at the center of the story does not care. This could be Jim, with his impotent frustration and general ineptness at being able to deal with shit, physically taking it out on his loved one, or this could be Lou himself, lamenting the same, and making sure Bettye knows about it.

Musically, the track is pushed along by the brass, anchored by Michael and Randy Brecker, along with Jon Pierson, who makes clear statements on bass trombone. This roars along, accented by menacing guitar spurts, until a long fade begins. What rises up in replacement is the song's return to its origins. By 3:30, all that remains is Lou and his acoustic guitar, asking 'how could you treat me this way'.

After the brash, angry declarations of the first part, this second section suggests the aftermath of chaos – the violence has passed, and Jim and Caroline are alone. In these bleak shadows where violence once reigned,

Caroline just has to know how Jim could treat her this way. 'Now you said that you loved us/ But you only made love to one of us' and then, once again, 'When you're looking through the eyes of hate'. Looking through the eyes of hate is an idea that could be applied to the art of Lou Reed as a whole. From an anxious, unsettled child at PS 192 in Brooklyn, to a troublesome and angry teen in Freeport, LI, and the nightmarish repercussions he had to face, to the many well-documented episodes from his professional career, strife and difficulty can be seen as Lou's regular companions, beyond other seemingly meaningful attachments and distractions, both artistically and personally. This song explores a great deal of emotional terrain, and once again, we must ask who it is that is really singing to us.

'Caroline Says II' (Reed)
At the start of side two of the LP, we hear from Caroline for the second time. This song shares a direct and consistent connection to the previous track. It also shares the most direct connection and similarity to Lou's first 'says' song, 'Stephanie Says', in both basic chords and melody, as well as recycled lyrical ideas. This song is a bummer; the first of a four-string bummer that is the second half of this album. It starts with picked acoustic guitar, with bits of drum and bass guitar added when needed. This is the core instrumentation for the track, save for vivid and ghostly mellotron and piano – played by Bob Ezrin – added in the middle to complement the song perfectly. This song seems to pick up right from where the previous left off; Caroline, 'as she gets up off the floor', asks why it is that she is beaten, and just to be clear, adds that 'it isn't any fun'. She also suggests that her perpetrator, Jim, '…learn more about yourself/Think more than just I', suggesting that she has some kind of an inkling as to what is behind Jim's violent madness. The chorus, closely resembling the same section in 'Stephanie Says', shifts the mood just a little: 'But she's not afraid to die/ All of her friends call her Alaska/When she takes speed, they laugh and ask her/What is in her mind.' Lou's vocals neither promote nor defeat the song; they are as functional as they need to be. The song ends with Caroline putting her fist through a windowpane, with the effect described as '…such a funny feeling', and then, finally, 'It's so cold in Alaska'.

'The Kids' (Reed)
Bloody Hell, this song. This largely acoustic number, strummed rhythm guitars and acoustic slide, joined by bass and drums, is, despite its gentle instrumentation, perhaps the most harrowing track on the album, or at the very least, it shares that honor with the next song – the verdict is still out. Lou's closely-mic'd voice casually utters a tale of a woman whose daughters have been taken away from her by the authorities '…because they said she was not a good mother'. Various one-line examples of this woman's sexual promiscuity are lined up and addressed, as well as drug use, compounded

by the fact that this woman had no compunction regarding the appropriate time or place for such interludes. Lou's voice curls into a gritted growl as he sings 'That miserable rotten slut couldn't turn anyone away'. Most of the goings-on in this song are observational; the singer/narrator telling us about what has happened, yet, curiously, the narrator gets to weigh in at the bridge, and the perspective is curious: 'And I am the Water Boy/The real game's not over here/But my heart is overflowing anyway.' This seeming bit of concern is thusly negated in the next set of lines: 'I'm just a tired man, no words to say/But since she lost her daughter/It's her eyes that fill with water/And I am much happier this way'. It has so far not been suggested in the narrative that the characters Jim and Caroline have children, but children are mentioned in the following track.

In John Cale's autobiography, *What's Welsh For Zen,* with Victor Bockris, Cale briefly mentions a former sex and drugs friend that he and Lou would visit in the early, pre-VU days in NYC, and due to her unique qualities and personality, they tried to get her to be in the band they were attempting to form. Her name was Daryl, and Cale, who had a sexual relationship with her, as did Lou, describes her as 'a nymphomaniac'. Heroin use and violence were often taking place at her apartment, to the extent to where her own two children were removed by the welfare authorities. Cale describes these scenes as '...part of the background of Lou's album *Berlin*'.

Musically, the song is excellent. The opening strumming guitar sets up a rhythm that is shambling yet sure, ragged but right. Procol Harum's BJ Wilson is on drums here, and his work is exemplary. He desperately stabs at the rhythm, occasionally landing a 'wrong' hit on the snare or bass drum that only pushes the falling-apartness of the song to greater heights. His work on this track cannot be overpraised. And then there are the kids, the actual children, who contribute to the vocals. Oft-recycled rumor states that these are in fact Bob Ezrin's children, who were brought to the studio and somewhat sketchily coaxed into their performance by being told that they would never see their mother again. With this in mind, the end results are not surprising, but by God, what a performance. The sheer horror of hearing these young children cry and call out for their mother, although deeply unsettling, is a true masterstroke in effectiveness, and it cements the song's narrative irrevocably. It's no goddamned fun to listen to, to be sure, but it works, all seven minutes and 55 seconds of it. With all of this in mind, it is an incredible song.

'The Bed' (Reed)

The pathos is unrelenting as we move from tragedy to tragedy. This song features yet another acoustic guitar intro, and Ezrin's production must once again be celebrated here, as the plucked notes just soar and weave in the rich, spacious sonic atmosphere that the producer has crafted. When Lou comes in, once again just barely above a whisper, his voice is another color added to the aural panoply. The singer, presumably Jim, faces the ghastly task of assessing the before and after of the bedroom he shared with Caroline in the wake of her suicide. 'This is the place where she lay her head' and 'This is the place where our children were conceived', serve to record the singer taking grim stock of the history the room holds. The unavoidable truth of the scene is addressed equally: 'And this is the place where she cut her wrists/that odd and fateful night'. The one time the singer moves beyond stark reportage is when he allows himself to personally weigh in on the proceedings, and he does so with puzzling language: 'And I said oh, oh, oh, oh, oh, oh, oh, what a feeling'. This might seem cold, or at the very least, cavalier, but that is where Lou makes the greatest impact with a less-is-more approach. Beyond horror, rage, agony, and pain, how else could one react and respond to the suicide of a loved one beyond simply marveling at the very intensity of what you are feeling as a result? Such vivid and perhaps even conflicting emotions run so hot and hard at a time like this that the sufferer might not possess the ability to name them, let alone understand them. Perhaps the only thing that can be done is to recognize the sheer vastness of what you feel; oh, what a feeling, a feeling unable to be tethered to any kind of recognizable, nameable emotion as it is too raw and wild at the time. Contrastingly, as there is always contrast with Lou, the bridge gives us 'I never would have started if I'd known/that it'd end this way/But funny thing I'm not at all sad/That it stopped this way' – huh? After running a detailed and harrowing catalog of the death scene's history, it is truly 'funny' that he is 'not at all sad' at how things turned out.

The instrumentation is once again sparse, but Gene Martynec deserves special credit for a vocal arrangement that is truly avant-garde. The singing and playing end at 4:45, and for the next minute-plus, the listener is bathed in a spectral chorus that waxes and wanes across the spectrum. It brings to mind the Greek folk song 'Tsintskaro', combined with György Legiti's 'Requiem II, Kyrie'. The swirling voices and tones suggest perhaps Caroline's spirit departing or the madness festering inside Jim's mind at the time. It is a haunting end to a truly haunting song.

'Sad Song' (Reed)

The last of the previous track's voices fade out to this song's opening chorus of flutes. This, the closing song, is the big production number, a Jack Nitzsche-like orchestral indulgence that ends these grim proceedings with a musical bang and is another much-revised hold-over from the *Loaded* era. Woods and strings lay a foundation as the singer describes the images of his late love in his picture book. Mary, Queen of Scots, is who she is compared to, as 'She seemed very regal to me/Just goes to show how wrong you can be'. The drums and guitars crash in for the singer to announce 'I'm gonna stop wasting my time/Somebody else would have broken both of her arms', at which point the rhythm pauses, the strings swirl about, and the singer speaks the song's title while a thick chorus sings the same behind him. Like all the tracks on this album, it is truly a sad song – does its title belabor the point? And while the ugly idea of repaying heartbreak with physical violence is nothing new, how valid is it when the heartbreaker in question is dead by her own hand? The song is lyrically sparse, and this allows the track to revel in its cinematic grandeur. It is perhaps overlong at nearly seven minutes, with repeated refrains and cadences, but this is the *Berlin* album at its close.

Rock 'n' Roll Animal (1974)

Personnel:
Lou Reed: vocals
Steve Hunter: guitar
Dick Wagner: guitar
Prakash John: bass
Pentii 'Whitey' Glan: drums
Ray Colcord: keyboards
Recorded at Howard Stein's Academy of Music, NYC, 21 December 1973
Producers: Steve Katz and Lou Reed
Engineer: Gus Mossler
Production Assistance: Bruce Somerfeld and Ralph Moss
Release Date: February 1974
Running Time: 40:32
Highest Chart Places: US: 45, UK: 26

Now that the 'concept' album is out of the way, it is time for that other 1970s milestone: the great, big 'live' album. Several musical careers were made with the great big 'live' album during the decade, and they often arrived as lifeboats to many acts that were floundering in commercial inertia due to their poor-selling previous studio albums. Like the 'concept' album, these 'live' albums were often hulking, two-LP sets, but not always, and just like *Berlin*, Lou's first and most commercially significant 'live' album is a single disc.

Recorded one night in December of 1973 in New York, this album, unlike many 'live' albums, is truly *live*, with no post-performance tweezing and tweaking in the studio, save for some airlifted audience sound – from a live John Denver LP, no less – due to one of the house mics conking out during recording. The recording's unretouched nature is clear upon listening; while the band is hot shit and razor-sharp, Lou's performance can be seen as erratic, to be charitable. Missed cues, fumbled entrances, and flubbed lyrics decorate this recording as souvenirs to rock 'n' roll's essences of spontaneity and immediacy, not to mention on-stage intoxication. Fronted by the double-barrel Detroit guitar juggernaut of Steve Hunter and Dick Wagner, bullied and burnished by Prakash John's undulating Rickenbacker bass, and kept fully grounded and forward-focused by Pentii 'Whitey' Glan's full-frontal drums and Ray Colcord's embroidery of tasteful and understated keyboards, this ensemble can do no wrong. It is little wonder that in roughly a year's time, Alice Cooper scooped up almost all the players for his first post-original band series of 'solo' albums.

As for the songs on offer, they are a curious selection. While this is ostensibly the tour for the *Berlin* album, this LP's original five tracks only feature one song from that album, 'Lady Day'. The remaining four songs are VU chestnuts, bearing little resemblance to their histories, all being given the 'showbiz' treatment. And that right there is the centre of the issues one could have with this album. While the LP was not only a commercial success, as well as a bad-ass rock 'n' roll classic, the greatest and most valid criticism to be levied here is that the souped-up and hot-rodded versions of the older material amount to little more than 'VU, Vegas Style'. True believers who had weathered the storms of Lou's career thus far, as well as those among the newly christened cultural genre known as 'rock journalism' – who could count the towering and tempestuous Lester Bangs among their ranks – saw this musical shift as a betrayal of sorts. Given what the intelligentsia knows about what Lou is capable of, these puffed and polished re-makes are seen as little more than the products of laziness and apathy; their end goal being little more than lucrative. Presently, knee-deep in the 21st century, the idea of 'selling out' is not only celebrated but also encouraged as a prime directive for any kind of creative endeavor, but in 1974, again among the true believers, this was seen as scandalous, especially for an artist of such singular ability. As for where Lou was in any of this, we must consult the tale of the tape.

The commercial success of this album is something that Lou saw cynically, and this was compounded by the bitterness he was feeling as a result of the commercial failure of *Berlin*. He also, at the close of this tour, became very resentful of the critical and audience attention that the band, particularly guitar players Steve Hunter and Dick Wagner, were garnishing. He saw this as upstaging, yet due to the commercial success of the album, he was torn. If the band, independent of his presence, was garnering such regard, where was he? If his intensive, heartfelt, and much-belabored previous statement that was the *Berlin* album fell on deaf ears, yet his turbo-charged dusting-off and tidying up of past glories bore such golden fruit, where was the true artist in all of this? These difficult realizations were, of course, compounded by the emotional and chemically enhanced reality that was Lou's day-to-day existence. After the perceived failure of *Berlin*, the success of *Rock 'n' Roll Animal* put him back in the good graces of the public and the press. In terms of the next step, which options were feasible, and which were absurd?

'Intro/Sweet Jane' (Hunter/Reed)

For the first time in his solo career, Lou conceded a co-writing credit on a track, and here it goes most deservedly to the magisterial intro concocted by Steve Hunter. At the start, Dick Wagner, in the right channel, does most of the riffing as the band builds the tension up. At 3:11, after riffage aplenty, the whole band locks in on two sets of three chords, a final additional two chords, and then, like falling rocks, bludgeons the audience into the unmistakable four-note groove that is 'Sweet Jane'. The excitement is palpable; to be rewarded so thoroughly after such a dazzling introduction. At the third cycle of this essential chord sequence, the audience flares up with applause as Lou takes the stage, icy cool in his black leather, neatly shorn black hair, and enough black about his eyes to see death. A magical live moment, for once successfully captured on record: it *is* rock 'n' roll. Despite this lightning-in-a-bottle start, Lou completely fucks up his entrance to the song; in the left channel, Steve Hunter begins to saw off chunks of raw meat with his guitar. He gets about three bars in, squeezes out a high, soaring note, and is abruptly cut off by Lou warbling, 'Standin' on a CORNAH!' Ever the professional, Hunter dials down the volume a taste, lets out four more meager notes, and gets out of his boss' way. This sort of thing was apparently a common occurrence for this band of hardened pros, working with a singer and leader so frequently distracted. The groove thunders on through chorus and verse with nary a hiccup. Lou is now truly the frontman; he does not touch a guitar onstage, and he takes broad liberties with vocal and verse phrasing throughout the entire LP. This track saw much airplay on the FM stations at the time, and it can be said that the album's success and reputation rest primarily here with this song, and it is all justified squarely.

'Heroin' (Reed)

This is the track that perhaps suffers the most from its revised arrangement. A full six minutes longer than 'The Banana Album' original, what it makes up for in duration, it lacks in all else. The band is perfectly adept at playing the arrangement, to be sure, but it's just *too good*; that is to say, too polished. The pervasive sense of beautiful disaster that is so prevalent and necessary to the original is wholly absent here. While the band is able to reenact the changes of tempo that distinguish the original – and they do so with studied flawlessness that travel from dirge-like crawls to hyper-space navigation – that is all that remains. Missing are the blends of horror and apathy, doubt and conviction, filth and finesse that so greatly signify the song itself. What we are left with is a sense of mere exercise. At one point during one of the many sections of increased tempo, Steve Hunter, who constructed this version's arrangement, bolsters the song's progress with what can only be described as a classic 1970s 'WHACK-a-CHICK-a, WHACK-a-CHICK-a' guitar rhythm, fully and richly enhanced with an MXR Phase 100. It could almost go disco, really. At 4:20, Ray Colcord gets a moment in the sun with a very Toccata and Fugue-esque organ break that adds to the flavor nicely, but at the end, the listener is left with a reading and rendition that, despite its technical expertise, is merely workmanlike in its glaring sheen.

'White Light/White Heat' (Reed)

This track is almost comical in its transformation. Starting with biting power chords from Hunter to set off the machine-driven tempo, Wagner adds slide snarls and the rest of the players fall in. Prakash John's burbling, percolating bass, all fingers and notes, greatly adds to the already strong locomotive action. Lou shouts out the words with a sense of drive; this is especially evident in the chorus where he barks the words like a frustrated coach goading his errant players from the sidelines. Again, the tempo is rugged and perfectly sustained, but comparing this version with the sensory blitzkrieg of the original is almost laughably moot. Truly, an 'apples and oranges' comparison, and for those of us who deeply cherish the original, this version is left standing.

'Lady Day' (Reed)
After 'Sweet Jane', this is the second most successful track on the album, which is interesting as it is the sole representative of the *Berlin* album. Like all other tracks on this album, this song gets a full structural and tonal makeover, yet your author would like to suggest that this version is an improvement on the original, as sacrilegious as that may seem. The sadness and desperation of the song are honoured here, as they should be, but this storming rock 'n' roll version sets these ideas alight in high relief. The rhythm section pounds and thuds with appropriate authority, and the guitars do what the guitars do throughout this album. It is Lou himself who distinguishes this song so. His emotional commitment to this recording has been strong and clear from the outset, despite technical deficiencies. When he spits out '... it had to be that way', you truly understand that it had to be that way. At the chorus, simple language centered around pure negation, Lou cannot be more clear in his rawness of intent as he roars out, 'No, no, no/oh Lady Day'. This song is his finest performance on the album.

'Rock 'n' Roll' (Reed)
Like 'Sweet Jane', a song of this magnitude is hard to fuck up, and they certainly do not do that here. If anything, this LP's closer can be accused of taking it just a bit too far, or perhaps too long. At 4:18, the basic song ends, and the gradual build-up to 'And it was alright' begins. This version, twice the length of the *Loaded* original, does not lack end-of-show pageantry, as the guitars glide and weave their way toward the song's concluding apex. Steve Hunter is given the spot as he grinds and shimmies out a busy rhythm that gradually allows the rest of the band back in with grand affair to close the proceedings. Things rant and rave for a total of ten minutes, which is plenty, and the album concludes with a surplus of audience enthusiasm.

Bonus Tracks
More recent reissues of this album have been amended with two bonus tracks, and the songs both hale from the *Berlin* album. As is often the nature with bonus tracks, their resignation to 'bonus' territory can be clearly determined upon listening, as both of these performances are merely perfunctory.

'How Do You Think it Feels?' (Reed)
As the track with the blatantly sleaziest vibe on *Berlin*, here it seems clumsy and malnourished. The tempo has been doubled from the original's gutter-crawl pace, and Lou sounds like he has no idea where to pitch his voice among the notes.

'Caroline Says I' (Reed)

This one is a bit more sure-footed, despite Lou blatantly blowing his lyrics right out of the starting gate. The song's foundation is provided by Ray Colcord on organ, and the guitars are given ample space to be guitars. Not much else happens here, save for one of Lou's classic 'SHADDAP!' admonitions to the audience between the numbers. These two bonus songs are usually placed between what would be the end of side one and the start of side two of the original LP, which aids the overall flow of the recording.

Sally Can't Dance (1974)

Personnel:
Lou Reed: vocals, acoustic guitar on 'Billy'
Danny Weis: guitar, tambourine, backing vocals, horn arrangement
Paul Fleisher: saxophone on 'Billy'
David Taylor, Lou Marini, Trevor Koehler, Jon Faddis, Alan Rubin, Alex Foster,
Lew Soloff: horns
Steve Katz: harmonica, horn arrangement
Michael Fonfara: piano, keyboards, mellotron on 'Ennui'
Prakash John: bass guitar, backing vocals
Doug Yule: bass guitar on 'Billy'
Ritchie Dharma: drums on 'Kill Your Sons' and 'Ennui'
Pentii 'Whitey' Glan: drums
Doug Bartenfeld: guitar
Michael Wendroff: backing vocals
Joanne Vent: backing vocals
Lew Soloff and Martin Sheller: horn arrangements
Produced at: Electric Lady Studios, New York, by Steve Katz and Lou Reed
Engineer: Mike Stone
Remix: Ralph Moss
Release Date: August 1974
Running Time: 32:58
Highest Chart Places: US: 10, UK: did not chart

What started out to be an honest-to-goodness R'n'B album, as well as the
first of Lou's solo albums recorded in NYC, it gradually went off the rails in
his hands, and its final manifestation can be credited to producer Steve Katz:
guitarist and founding member of Blood, Sweat, and Tears, brother of soon-
to-be-acrimoniously (and expensively) ousted manager Dennis Katz, and the
producer of the previous successful live album, *Rock 'n' Roll Animal*. How the
end product can be gauged is purely in the realm of the listener; with that
being said, this is an album of interesting firsts.

As previously mentioned, this was Lou's first solo LP actually born and
bred in New York, and it is also the first to feature Michael Fonfara on
keyboards, who would figure prominently in Lou's works and bands for the
duration of the decade, rising to the level of band leader, and even receiving
co-writing credits on certain songs for his trouble. Additionally, the back
cover image, reflected in Lou's sunglasses, features an individual, credited
as René De La Bush, who would be a central and influential person in Lou's
life for the next several years. Not only would she become manager of his
personal affairs, but also a radiant, romantic partner who would inspire him
to explore vast polar opposites in his work, from the banal to the brilliant,
and set eyebrows arching and tongues wagging from pillar to post. Coasting
on the fumes of *Rock 'n' Roll Animal*, this is also the first, and only, Lou LP

to enter the top ten, despite critical drubbing and an unsuccessful title-track single. It is also the album that Lou would disparage the most, retrospectively, a process already becoming habitual at this point. Furthermore, it would continue nearly unabated throughout his career, with regard to not only albums but also former bandmates, managers, lovers, and anyone else who fell within the searchlight sweep of his scattershot wrath.

As stated, this record went into the top ten album charts despite lacking a successful single, as well as Lou's heavily medicated lack of personal involvement. As Steve Katz was ultimately responsible for pulling a finished product together, he would, like so many others, earn Lou's resentment on account of Lou losing his sense of control, and someone else making decisions on his, and the album's, behalf. Never mind that the record was a real hit; this did not matter after Lou put so much into *Berlin* only to see it spat on by critics and the public alike. So, why try? If he could just show up to the studio, whip out his lyrics, be pointed toward the microphone, and be a guaranteed success, what did it matter? We would soon see just precisely how much or how little it would or could matter. Critics, ever eager to pounce on an artist of real substance while they are down, saw this album's commercial success, combined with the success of *Rock 'N' Roll Animal*, as Lou's further betrayal of his true abilities. While it is by no means one of Lou's best albums, it is a pretty tight and greasy 1970s New York rock 'n' roll album, in spite of itself. Curiously, the same can be said of the final VU album, *Loaded*, with which it shares certain similarities. Both records feature their artistic creator functioning under reduced circumstances: for *Sally Can't Dance*, it's drugs; for *Loaded*, it's crushing depression, resulting in Lou quitting the band before the album's completion. And just like *Sally*, while *Loaded* is by no means any kind of VU masterstroke, it is a rip-shittin' New York City 1970s rock 'n' roll album as it stands. Both albums achieve a similar status and functionality, despite all their amputations.

'Ride Sally Ride' (Reed)

A gentle dialog between piano and French horn starts things off, and soon Lou enters, inviting the listener to 'Sit yourself down...' Guitarist Denny Weis introduces himself with tasty riffs that glide in smoothly due to manipulation of the volume knob of his Telecaster. As this album will show, Lou has found himself another hot shit guitarist; he will pass through the ranks all too soon. Things chug along in an uncomplicated, laid-back vibe when we come to the chorus. 'Ride Sally Ride/It's not your time or way of confusion' suggests a narrative anchor for the lyrics, but in the next set of lines, Lou commits the cardinal sin of rhyming 'confusion' with 'contusion'. Didn't they teach him better at Syracuse? Little matter here, as the chorus concludes with what could be one of the Lou-est of Lou Reed lines ever: 'Oohh isn't it nice when you find your heart's made out of ice'. By 2:40, the lyrics have been fully cycled and recycled through, and for the last minute and a half, the band works its way through a musical cadence that attempts to bring this album's R'n'B bona fides to the fore. Handclaps, horn section blasts, and expressive background singers all fulfill their obligations to elevate and then close the song. A curious low-key and low pulse start to the album.

'Animal Language' (Reed)

This one is an oddity. If the lyrics are to be taken literally, they are among the most banal and tossed-off (but still with a twist of their own, as per anything with Lou) of anything in Lou's catalog. If the lyrics are to be taken metaphorically, then their anthropomorphic characters are simply having fun with drugs. Who can say? The band cooks up and maintains a busy, active groove, with Denny Weis launching bright, yet tasteful guitar spurts between verses. And what verses they are. Miss Riley, the dog owner, must cope with the loss of her dog getting shot down its throat as a result of her disgruntled neighbors being fed up with the dog's constant barking. Similarly, Miss Murphy, the cat owner, must contend with the loss of her cat as a result of a blood clot due to 'overheating'. Fascinating stuff. The narrative apex appears in the third stanza:

> Then the dog met the cat, the dog was hot and the cat was wet
> Then in came some sweaty dude, he put a board between the two
> Then they couldn't get at it, got frustrated all about it
> So they did the only thing you could do
> They took the dude's sweat and shot it up between the two

What does, or can, this actually mean? One of the truly rewarding things about appreciating any kind of 'other' culture is the frequently recurring, multi-tiered question of 'Is this real/Is this surreal; Is this serious/Is this a joke'. This series of questions can be applied to anything under the sun (or moon): the films of Doris Wishman or Herschell Gordon Lewis, the music of The Shaggs (the Massachusetts Shaggs, not the Illinois Shaggs), or The Godz (the NYC Godz, not the Ohio Godz), among a gratifyingly endless set of additional examples. Any kind of art that teeters along the ledge of the 'is this good/is this bad' conundrum is often the richest and most consistently challenging stuff to be perceived, simply due to the fact that easy and comfortable categorization is not an option. Does 'Animal Language' belong here, among such puzzling, high and exalted company? That large decision rests, as only it could, with the listener.

'Baby Face' (Reed)

'Jim, living with you's not such fun, you're not the only one', is what starts off this tale of lovers' woe, the lovers here being, it is assumed, two men. The band achieves a quiet, yet crucial groove; what it lacks in bright bombast, it surpluses in a smoldering simmer, and keeps it that way. Again, Denny Weis responds to Lou's verses with verses of his own on guitar, pound for pound. While the narrator goes through his list of his lover's deficiencies, a curious thing happens: a ghostly, reverb-enhanced voice adds real-time drama to the proceedings: 'Man you never split your stash or your bread' eventually followed by 'You can keep it/JUST KEEP IT', voiced by an unnamed character to add an element of mysterious presence to the song.

'N.Y. Stars' (Reed)

For an album that began as an R'n'B project, the funk finally appears at the close of the album's first side. A deeply gut-bucket guitar riff slaps against a glottal cowbell to start this song. What follows is a bitter, thoroughly jaded account of an impression of Lou's fans who have endeavored to remake themselves in their singer's image: 'The faggot mimic machine never had ideas/Mission impossible they self-destruct on their fears', and 'On a standard New York night/Ghouls go to see their so-called stars'. Michael Fonfara distinguishes himself with busy, propulsive clavinet as Lou lays waste to his fanboys. He does no actual singing on this track, as his vocals are confined to deep, double-tracked murmur. Despite a noncommittal performance, the lyrics get fairly descriptive: 'Like new buildings/Square, tall and the same/ Sorry Ms. Stupid/Didn't know you didn't know it's a game'. While these sentiments belong to the past era of tabloid supremacy, they could just as easily apply to the current era of social media status and embellishment, with all its worshipful and imitative fits and starts.

'Kill Your Sons' (Reed)

Even in the very depths of Lou's worst, most cringe-worthy albums, there is always at least one flake of gold among the hill of dross; at least your author thinks so, and while *Sally Can't Dance* is not exactly Lou's worst, it is at the low end of the totem pole if only due to a sheer quantitative absence of its creator. With that having been said, 'Kill Your Sons' shines out like a beaming ray of golden light. It starts off side two of this album with a massive serving of 1970s sleaze. Ritchie Dharma's plodding one-two drums anchor things down, along with Michael Fonfara's organ chords keeping tone. On bass, Prakash John peps things up a bit with his customary fluidity, but it is Deny Weis who really soars on this track, with his sustained, full-throttle guitar runs. His playing reaches a high point in the chorus, where he duets with Lou's vocals as they both descend the musical scale.

And then, there are the lyrics. Beginning as an acoustic demo in 1971 with completely different lyrics that railed against political corruption and the Vietnam War, this revised and recharged version allows the listener to peer into raw personal history. As with any work of Lou's that suggests autobiography, this is a mixed bag; some of it is factual, some of it embellishment. The first set of verses is true to life, where Lou recalls his time spent in New York psychiatric institutions as a teen, receiving electroconvulsive therapy for his mental health issues.

> All your two-bit psychiatrists are giving you electric shock
> They said they'd let you live at home with Mom and Dad
> Instead of mental hospitals
> But every time you tried to read a book you couldn't
> Get to page seventeen
> 'Cause you forgot where you were
> So you couldn't even read

It has long been speculated that one of the key reasons, if not *the* key reason, that his parents followed their family doctor's advice on such a procedure was an attempt to 'cure' Lou of his homosexual orientation, yet Lou's sister, Dr. Merrill Reed Weiner, with whom Lou was consistently close throughout his life, has discredited these ideas as recently as 2021 in Todd Haynes' *The Velvet Underground: A Documentary*. She reminds the viewer that this was happening on Long Island, NY, in 1959; not only were things drastically less tolerant, but also people typically followed their doctor's orders without much question. She also makes very clear the crushing, lifelong guilt both her parents carried to their graves as a result of the disastrous effects that their attempts to help their son ultimately resulted in. Throughout his life, Lou frequently laid blame and spite at his parents' feet, seeing them as both original sources and continuing contributors to whatever his *misère du jour* might be. Regardless, it's chilling stuff, with its matter-of-fact examples of how ECT completely singes the memory of the patient, and the namechecking of two of the New York institutions that Lou was a patient of: Creedmore Psychiatric Center in Queens, and Payne Whitney Psychiatric Hospital in Manhattan. In the Todd Haynes film, Dr. Reed Weiner also states that separating fact from fiction in Lou's work is a challenging task, and this cannot be clearer in the second set of verses. At the time, Lou was kind enough to give his sister fair warning about her presence on his new album, and how despite the fact that none of it was true, it rhymed, and that was what he needed at the moment of composition:

> Mom informed me on the phone she didn't know what to do about dad
> He took an axe and broke the table, aren't you glad you're married
> And sister she got married on the Island
> and her husband takes the train
> He's big and he's fat – and he doesn't have a brain

Apparently, the only actual truthful statement in that section is that Merrill did indeed get married on Long Island at the time. The rest is embroidery, and she struggled to make peace with it, despite her brother's pre-album release consideration.

'Ennui' (Reed)

From the horrors of psychiatric difficulty, we move to this moody ballad in an existential vein. 'Ah, you're getting old, you're doing things/You're losing your hair'; could these be directed to the image seen in the mirror, or are they just another one of Lou's many collages of characters on the streets? The band floats along easily, with Denny Weis' volume-controlled guitar sounding more like a pedal steel, and Michael Fonfara elevating the drama with his mellotron-produced chorus in the middle of the song. As for what's on Lou's mind, it is never settled. 'They live without any talent or fun/Running out in the streets/Balling anyone/It's the truth' and more curiously, 'You're the kind of person that I could do without/ Certain kinds of money/Would make you see what it's all about'. This seeming call to self-revision has an air of effete exhaustion to it, and it could be directed at multiple targets both within and without the narrator.

'Sally Can't Dance' (Reed)

The title track opens up the party with slippery funk and nasty words. The band busts it out with ease, as Michael Fonfara's double-barrel clavinet and organ roll and rollick, accompanied by Prakash John's smooth, bumpy bass. For the second time on this album, the first being 'Kill Your Sons', Lou steps up to the mic and seems to give a shit with his delivery; a rarity for an album that saw him so consistently checked out. Sally appears to be a composite of people, with Lou's erstwhile vocalist Nico getting a share of the narrator's attention with the lines:

Sally became a big model
She moved up to Eightieth and Park
She had a studio apartment
And that's where she used to ball folk singers

This is seen as a reference to Nico's pre-VU years as an actor and model, and her immediate post-VU days, as she tried her hands at various solo vocal gigs, often backed on guitar by young boys of the town. Jackson Browne was one of these accompanists/lovers, as were both Lou and Sterling Morison, among others. The other lines are not pretty. Sally is 'losing her face', she met her demise 'in the trunk of a Ford', and 'She took too much meth and can't get off of the floor', to name a few. But the worst is saved for the bridge:

She was the first girl in her neighborhood
Who got raped in Tomkins Square
Real good

Now, she wears a sword like Napoleon
And she kills the boys and acts like a son

That's rough, but that's Lou; he is merely reporting, as he would tell you, but the 'real good' that describes sexual assault is of another category entirely. A neutered and cauterized remake of this song, without any troublesome language, or for that matter, muscle to the groove, was released as a single, but not only did it fail to trouble the charts, it also had no impact on the LP's rise to the top ten.

'Billy' (Reed)
The album's acoustic closer sees a few interesting changes. For one, Lou rediscovers his guitar, and he bangs out the chords while he sings – just like the old days. And, speaking of old days, the bass is handled by none other than Doug Yule, who has seemingly been welcomed in from the cold after squeezing, literally and figuratively, every last drop he could from the carcass of the VU. The two players are augmented by Paul Fleisher's sax colorations on this sorrowful tale of two youthful paths diverging. The singer and Billy were friends since age nine, and as they went on, Billy played football and attended to his studies, while the singer did not. Additionally, Billy was successful in college – the singer, not. Ultimately, Billy, despite being a doctor, is called off to Vietnam, and he returns a mere shell of himself, leaving the singer to ponder, 'Now I often wonder which one of us was the fool'. It is a sentimental, three-chord closing statement to the album that is really given life by the lyrical and vocal sax playing.

Bonus Tracks
'Sally Can't Dance' (Reed)
This bonus version is an exclusive re-recording of the song, as opposed to a remix of the album track, created as a 'radio-friendly' version that omits any 'troublesome' language. It also omits any trace of funk, fun, or pulse of the original, and as a single failed to chart.

'Good Taste' (Reed)
This track is flooded with reverb that sonically differentiates itself from the rest of the LP, suggesting that this was left alone in the can and mixed after the fact for CD release. As a song, it plods along, with a stinging guitar solo by Denny Weis, while Lou suggests that the person 'making a fool of yourself/ by following me around' has, in fact, 'Good Taste'. His vocals could not be more downplayed; it is as if he had just woken up, approached the mic, and begun to recite lines.

Lou Reed Live (1975)

Personnel:
Lou Reed: vocals
Steve Hunter: guitar
Dick Wagner: guitar
Prakash John: bass
Pentii 'Whitey' Glan: drums
Ray Colcord: keyboards
Rob Hegel: background vocals on 'Sad Song'
Recorded at Howard Stein's Academy of Music, NYC, 21 December 1973
Producer: Steve Katz
Engineer: Gus Mossler
Production Assistance: Bruce Somerfeld and George Semkiw
Release Date: March 1975
Running Time: 37:49
Highest Chart Places: US: 62, UK: did not chart

A cash grab, to be sure. Lou had been making noise aplenty regarding his dissatisfaction with his management and his record label; by now, it should be obvious that this would not be the first nor the last issuance for either of these types of grievances. While this would not be his last album for RCA, nor his final album under the managerial tutelage of Dennis Katz, all parties were beginning to see the writing on the wall. Lou had begun what would become a long and costly separation from both manager and label at this time, and the professional and financial repercussions would leave lasting scars for all parties involved. As a result of what was perceived to be an impending storm, manager and label did what could only be seen as commercially sound: if *Rock 'n' Roll Animal* was so successful, why, here's some more, and like *Rock 'n' Roll Animal*, it is an excellent live rock 'n' roll album. The problem here is the aspect of subterfuge. Lou himself had no idea as to the genesis of this album, nor did the participant musicians. When Prakash John and Pentii Glan learned that RCA had no intention of paying them for their contributions to this recording, it served as the final straw of their employment with Lou Reed. In almost direct opposition to *Rock 'n' Roll Animal*, it features only one song from the good old days, 'I'm Waiting For the Man', and updates things with two songs from *Berlin* and three from *Transformer*. With all of this in mind, like *Rock 'n' Roll Animal*, it is a fine live tribute to a brutal, well-oiled rock 'n' roll band.

It's not such a bad album, really; an extension of the positive aspects of his first live album. This LP was, of course, even more fuel to the fire of those who claimed that Lou was just pissing in the wind with half-assed commercial products when he was clearly artistically capable of so much more. The fact that this LP was crafted and concocted without Lou's input, almost to its actual release, contributes to this derisive thinking. If they only knew what lay in store.

'Vicious' (Reed)
Things storm right out of the gate with this thumper; the guitar chords crunch in thick unison, and the crowd appreciates it. The first set of solo riffs belongs to Steve Hunter, and it is a curious alteration to this album's mix that sees Hunter in the right channel and Wagner in the left – it is the opposite on *Rock 'n' Roll Animal*. Prakash John continues to distinguish himself during the verses with bubbly, percolating Rickenbacker froth, and all the pieces fall together without complication. Lou shouts his words with a casual conviction – does he care, or doesn't he? Wrapping up at six minutes, it's a bit overlong, but it's a cracking party starter.

'Satellite of Love' (Reed)
This song suffers from a fairly watered-down reading that really lacks the sense of weightlessness that the studio version offers. Ray Colcord's heavily phased clavinet drives the song, and while distinct, is not on par with the gliding piano on *Transformer*. There are guitar riffs aplenty, as per usual, but Lou prances about through the lyrics in a way that once again suggests he has better things to do, at least according to him.

'Walk on the Wild Side' (Reed)
This one, regardless of the band, is hard to pull off live, simply because atmosphere is so crucial to the original. Prakash John admirably does the work of two basses, and he fires it up in the immediate aftermath of the previous song's conclusion. The band do their best to keep the tempo mellow and the vibe smooth, and they by and large succeed. Lou camps up the vocals like a low-rent Freddie Mercury, oooh-ing and aahh-ing at choice moments. The 'colored girls' are represented by members of the band who are uncredited with background vocals. The end result, while competent, is less than satisfying, and to our benefit, Lou would release superior live versions of this key number in years to come.

'I'm Waiting For the Man' (Reed)
Starting off the LP's second side, this VU chestnut truly benefits from the Hunter/Wagner band treatment. The song itself has been chopped and channeled, rinsed and repeated so many times in so many ways, often by its own creators, that a sense of allowance is afforded to it, and this version truly fucks shit up. Starting with tom-tom thunder and bristling clavinet, things are pumping on all cylinders, waiting for the man to tell his very truthful and accurate story of what it's like to try and score drugs in potentially hostile territory. Lou seems more engaged here, positively roaring certain lines, 'FEEL SICK AND DIRTY!' and allowing the unfinished verse to stand on its own. Hunter and Wagner offer no solos here, as they are interlocked in brutal, metal-scraping-metal string work that perfectly complements the crushing rhythm section. This song is the album's stand-out cut.

'Oh Jim' (Reed)

The last two songs on the album are the most contemporary, as they hail from the *Berlin* album. At ten minutes and 40 seconds, it is this album's longest track, and the band does a solid job of bringing the song's drama and pageantry to the stage. At two minutes and 33 seconds, the band steps into an extended musical section that rises and falls with each player's contributions, driven by cowbell rings and dual rhythm guitar snarls. Steve Hunter gets a moment in the spotlight with a busy guitar solo that sneaks in at 3:39 and meanders purposefully until the baton is effortlessly passed to Dick Wagner at 5:18. At 5:36, they trade fours back and forth, elevating the musical tension accordingly. The pyrotechnics start to die down by 7:20, and at 7:44, Pentii Glan taps out the rhythm to the song's second part on the bell of the ride cymbal. All other instruments come out of the post-jam fog and fall into place. At last, at 8:37, the singer returns to ask Jim how they could be treated this way. Lou sings it with balls, and the atmosphere onstage is palpable. Things die down to just Wagner's granite chord raunch and the singer talking about looking through the eyes of hate. They are briefly joined by Hunter, adding trills and bits, and things ultimately land with ease, creating a space for the final song on the album.

'Sad Song' (Reed)

As it is the closing song on its album of origin, it is here as well. Ray Colcord briskly rises from the remains of the previous song, playing the flute chorus of the original on the organ, which serves as the anchor to the whole performance, as it does on the version from *Berlin*. The rest of the band does a respectable job of replacing the original track's orchestration with their rock 'n' roll apparatus. Lou enters, not so much singing as announcing: it's the end of the show, the end of the album, the end of the story. The rhythm section establishes and maintains a solid thudding pace that makes up for what is lost from the orchestral grandeur of the studio version. At the song's chorus, background vocalists reappear to sing the song's title, yet this song sees an exclusive credit to Rob Hegel on background vocals on this track alone, which suggests a post-concert overdub in the studio, defying these recordings' reputations as unretouched sonic documents. At 4:26, the extended coda begins which will lead to the song's conclusion, replete with a blistering Dick Wagner solo. The band rests and the final notes dissipate at 7:10, and the diligent, patient listener will be rewarded at 7:27 in the left channel, as a member of the crowd loudly exclaims, 'Lou Reed Sucks!' The inclusion was apparently insisted upon by Lou himself in order for the album to see completion and release.

Metal Machine Music/The Amine β Ring (1975)

Personnel:
Lou Reed: all the sounds
Producer: Lou Reed
Release Date: July 1975
Running Time: 64:11/ ∞
Highest Chart Places: did not chart, withdrawn after three weeks

OK, so it's time to talk about *that* album. What can be said? Is there anything left to be said? Your author maintains a position in the affirmative. It has a reputation singularly its own in the history of pop music/pop culture. Its intentions, while multi-limbed, have never been squarely resolved, and Lou being Lou, they have been known to change over time. Is it an attempt at commodified exorcism? A glaring and violent stab at liberation from the confines of commercial success and all its trappings? Is it a bold, creative, avant-garde statement, a post-music declaration of, and salutation to, the leisure of the future? Is it a loud and spiteful 'FUCK YOU' to manager, label, public, reputation, the past, etc.? Yes. Yes, it is.

Released in the summer of 1975 after a string of three very successful releases, this four-sided cacophony could not have been more jarring. Lou's label, RCA, had flirted with the idea of releasing it on their Red Seal label, which was used for compositional and orchestral releases. Whether this was seen as label brass truly 'believing' in the 'product', as industry parlance goes, or whether this was an attempt to bury what could be nothing but a commercial failure of an album in the wastes of 'niche' marketing, the idea was shot down by Lou himself, who believed it would be commercially and artistically inappropriate. Why relegate a vital creative piece of art like this to the 'specialty nerd' section at the back of the record store, while *Rock 'n' Roll Animal* and *Sally Can't Dance* were readily available in the bins at the front? It is a valid artistic and egalitarian point, to be sure.

So, what *is* it? Simply put, it is a double LP of four sides of chaotic electronic sound, generated, we are told, by Lou in his apartment, using electric guitars, amps, and sustained loops of the feedback that these instruments produced. The LP's front cover shows our Lou onstage in leather and shades, as does the rear cover, perhaps giving the buyer the illusion that this was yet another live album. Not quite. Sides one through three of the original vinyl were programmed to last an equal duration of 16:01, with the fourth side being pressed in a 'locked groove' format that allows the last musical revolution of the album at the disc's center to repeat endlessly until the listener physically causes it to stop. The album sides do not actually measure out to such strict duration, but it probably does not matter. On all four sides, there is a wash of howling, screaming electronic sound, rigidly split down the center of the stereo spectrum, with noticeably and obviously different sounds in either channel. As the listener goes from side one to side four, if they choose to, there are oscillations and variations of pitch, tone, and timbre throughout. These can be heard frequently even if the listener relegates themselves to one side at a time; on the rather expansive liner notes, Lou himself indicates that he himself has not listened to the whole thing from start to finish, nor has anyone he knows, although your author did, in fact, do such a thing, several times before, during, and since, in preparation for this book, among other reasons.

Apart from the music inside (and your author does indeed consider this *music*, which is not a universally held belief), the liner notes must be given special attention, not only for what they disclose but also for what they conceal. At the top of the back cover is a long and detailed list of the various machines and materials used in the recording. There are some typical rock 'n' roll ingredients listed, such as '5 (!) piggyback Marshall Tube Amps in series', 'Sunn Tremolo Unit', 'Fender Dual Showman Bass Amp with Reverb Unit' specified as '(Pre-Columbia)', affirming its vintage significance, as well as 'Arbitor distortor (sic) (Jimi's)', the classic 'Fuzz Face' distortion pedal that Hendrix made famous. There are also references to LaMonte Young and his work with drones, which Lou often cited as an inspiration for this album, as well as a brief list of what is *not* featured in the recording: 'No Synthesizers. No Arp. No Instruments?', and further down, 'No panning. No phasing', and finally, obliquely, 'No'. Never one to skip a technical detail, the album's credits conclude with the chemical symbol of the Benzedrine drug cluster, as described by Aidan Levy in his Lou biography *Dirty Blvd*:

Subtitled 'The Amine β Ring: An Electronic Instrumental Composition', it referenced amine, an ammonia derivative used to make meth, β-Methylphenethylamine, meth's positional isomer, and the ring, both a chemical property as well as a sound modulator. An asterisk above the subtitle pointed to 'dextrorotary components synthesis of sympathomimetic musics', alluding to D-methamphetamine, a potent psychostimulant and sympathomimetic drug.

Lou has often gone on record declaring that he was truly high as fuck when he made this album. But is that all this is? The product of a stoned, successful malcontent, lashing out at the demands that his job places on him? At the time of the album's creation, Lou had already been working on what would be its follow-up LP, *Coney Island Baby*, but work had stalled for a number of reasons. His contract with RCA was for two complete releases a year, and despite his frequent success, they came a-calling for their next pound of flesh, and Lou was working very slowly. He did not have enough completed songs for a full LP due to the fact that most of his time was spent pumping himself full of speed and snapping and preserving Polaroid pictures of the various trans persons and other nocturnal denizens that were his peers during his urban after-dark club crawls. The lawyers also began knocking, as Lou had just lost a case for a settlement against his former manager Fred Heller, who was summarily dismissed in 1971 to make room for Dennis Katz, who was now also about to be very expensively shown the door as well. Lou's father Sidney, an accountant by trade, had advised Lou to settle with Heller years previously as it seemed like the cleanest and quickest way to resolve this business dispute. Surprising no one, Lou refused, and a judge ruled on a massively increased fee from the original settlement sum. Then, there were also 'the kids'; the bleary-eyed, quaalude-and-wine teens who bought his last two or three albums and flocked to his concerts, only to ignore the words and wonder aloud about what the fuck had happened to Dick and Steve.

With the aforementioned stressors, it is easy to see *Metal Machine Music* as the great big 'FUCK YOU' it has often been described as. Lou himself has given credence to this theory, but what if he actually really did 'mean it', as he has also repeatedly urged? In interviews at the time, he mentioned listening to the music of Romanian-born composer Giannis Klearchou Xenakis, known for using modes of mathematics in composition and architecture, among many other experimental modes of creation and design. Lou also claimed that deep within the tonal bowels of *MMM*, he had placed elements of the *Eroica* and *Pastoral* symphonies of Beethoven, as well as Mozart and/or Bach (Frank Zappa made similar claims as to hidden elements of Stravinsky buried deep within the saccharine doo-wop of his *Cruising With Ruben and the Jets* LP). At later points in the future, Lou refuted the above claims, or reinforced them, according to whim. Perhaps the clearest picture we can get is from the original LP's liner notes, which begin on the front cover and conclude in the center gatefold. They are reproduced here in full:

When I started the Velvet Underground and its various spring-offs, my concern was not, as was assumed abidingly lyrical, verbally oriented at heart, 'head' rock, the exploration of various 'taboo' subjects drugs, sex violence ... passion – REALISM – realism was the key. The records were letters. Real letters from me to certain other people. Who had and still have basically, no music, be it verbal or instrumental, to listen to. One of the peripheral effects, typically distorted, was what was to be known as heavy metal rock. In reality, it was of course, diffuse, obtuse, weak, boring and, ultimately, an embarrassment. This record is not for parties/dancing/background, romance. This is what I meant about 'real' rock, about 'real' things. No one I know has listened to it all the way through, including myself. It is not meant to be. Start any place you like. Symmetry, mathematical precision, obsessive and detailed accuracy and the vast advantage one has over 'modern electronic composers'. They, with neither sense of time, melody or emotion, manipulated or no. It's for a certain time and place of mind. It is the only recorded work I know of seriously done as well as possible as a gift, if one could call it that, from a part of certain head to a few others. Most of you

won't like this, and I don't blame you at all. It's not meant for you. At the
very least, I made it so I had something to listen to. Certainly Misunderstood;
Power to Consume (how Bathetic); an idea done respectfully, intelligently,
sympathetically and graciously, always with concentration on the first and
foremost goal. For that matter, off the record, I love and adore it. I'm sorry,
but not especially, if it turns you off. One record for us and it. I'd harbored
hope that the intelligence that once inhabited novels or films would ingest
rock. I was, perhaps, wrong. This is the reason *Sally Can't Dance* – your
Rock 'n' Roll Animal. More than a decent try, but hard for us to do badly.
Wrong media, unquestionably. This is not meant for the market. The
agreement one makes with 'speed'. A specific acknowledgment, A to say the
least, very limited market. *Rock 'n' Roll Animal* makes this possible, funnily
enough. The misrepresentation succeeds to the point of making possible the
appearance of the progenitor. For those of whom the needle is no more than
a toothbrush. Professionals, no sniffers please, don't confuse superiority (no
competition) with violence, power or other justifications. The Tacit speed
agreement with Self. We did not start World War I, II, or III. Or the Bay of
Pigs, for that Matter. Whenever. As way of disclaimer, I am forced to say that,
due to stimulation of various centers (remember OOOHHHMMM, etc.), the
possible negative contraindications must be pointed out. A record has to,
of all things Anyway, hypertense people, etc. possibility of epilepsy (petite
mal), psychic motor disorders, etc., etc., etc. My week beats your year.

He closes out with the absolute mother of all closers, 'My week beats your
year'. Of all the very Lou things Lou has uttered over his creative lifetime,
nothing out-Lous that one. He begins the broadside by mentioning the pursuit
of realism in his art; his lyrics are in fact, letters to actual people, people who
themselves lack music, lyrics, and voices of their own. As broad and sweeping
a statement as this may be, this is not at all a stretch to those of us who
have found meaning and reason in his music. He then goes on to describe
what the album is not meant to be used for, and despite the fact that you
may not like it, he is not terribly sorry, for he loves it. He also mentions his
previous two LPs, both commercial successes, with a dismissive tone, as if to
say that what is presented here, in *MMM,* is the pure, qualitative antidote for
the tawdry, market-based posturing of *Rock 'n' Roll Animal* and *Sally Can't
Dance.* He also, of course, makes mention of the crucial and central role that
speed plays in this album, from how it can aid as a listening enhancement
to actual directions for usage and administration (no sniffers, please). Lots to
unpack.

'Metal Machine Music A-1' (Reed)
'Metal Machine Music A-2' (Reed)
'Metal Machine Music A-3' (Reed)
'Metal Machine Music A-4' (Reed)

The ultimate assessment of *Metal Machine Music* rests, of course, with the listener. At the time of its release, the listeners were not having it, to the extent that customer returns to music stores were so pervasive that RCA felt compelled to issue a formal letter of apology to major retailers, before ultimately withdrawing the title from retail sales completely a mere three weeks after its initial release. This, naturally, enraged Lou, and he would use it as additional fuel to his fire of indignation at manager, label, etc. With regard to all of that, how do you, the reader/listener feel about this album? In spite of the amputations, to borrow a phrase, that is truly all that matters. With an album as challenging as this, it must be left up to each individual participant to assess their own true sense of value and worth to the sounds contained within. The questions start at the crucial juncture of whether or not this can actually be considered 'music' or not. Your author has already made his position clear, but so what? What truly defines 'music' is a vast, deep, and possibly unsolvable puzzle of manifold complexity. Where do we begin? Given that there are only twelve notes available to us on the chromatic scale, at this point knee-deep in the 21st century, is music actually dead? Have we, as a species, said all that can be said with this assortment of twelve tones? Valid and circuitous quandaries, yet the aim of this book is not to answer these types of questions but to talk about the music of Lou Reed. *Metal Machine Music* is most certainly noise; having made that clear, any kind of qualitative value we assign to noise is purely speculative. In an interview with Kristine McKenna from 1984, Brian Eno speaks of the listenability of noise as simply a matter of location to the source of the sound:

> If you listen to city noises up close, they are filled with angst and trauma and are hard to take. But if you listen to anything in the city from the right distance, it becomes a non-threatening hum. The sounds one hears in the country might seem quite lovely and pastoral, but those, too, are probably sounds of emergency. The little bird singing is probably sounding some kind of alarm, and the screeching monkey has probably lost his mother. So, it's really a question of your mental proximity to the source of the sounds you're hearing.

So, all you really need to do is have *MMM* at a low level on your earbuds while you pump away in spin class, or perhaps play it through your Alexa speaker in the back room while you attend to your life matters in the front room, right? It's really up to you. The aforementioned Xenakis, not to mention John Cage, Sun Ra, as well as countless others, have sought to address music in new and, at the same time, primordial elements throughout the twentieth century; *Metal Machine Music* is another station in that long train ride. In 1975, this was a lot to take from a *Top of the Pops* artist who had provable commodified status. In our present day, it is almost a rite of passage for a certain kind of artist who might want to shake off a few mid-career cobwebs.

Presently, *MMM* can be perceived as surprisingly listenable, depending on your personal variables, and like most shocking artistic statements, it has taken just a few decades to be truly appreciated.

Coney Island Baby (1975)

Personnel:
Lou Reed: vocals, rhythm guitar, piano
Bob Kulick: lead guitar, slide guitar
Bruce Yaw: bass guitar
Michael Suchorsky: drums, percussion
Joanne Vent, Michael Wendroff, Godfrey Diamond: backing vocals
Doug Yule: bass guitar (on CD bonus tracks)
Bob Meday: drums (on CD bonus tracks)
Michael Fonfara: keyboards (on CD bonus tracks)
Produced at: Mediasound, NYC, by Lou Reed and Godfrey Diamond
Recorded by: José Rodriguez
Release date: US: December 1975, UK: 19 January 1976
Running time: 35:15
Highest chart places: US: 41, UK: 52

Rising up phoenix-like from the ashes of noise and attitude, this musical love letter appeared at the top of the new year to try and put things to rights. While some mid-1975 demos were seen as a tentative start to his post-*MMM* commercial recovery, Lou had relieved Steve Katz from his producer's duties (resulting in a breach-of-contract lawsuit), as he was also attempting to sever managerial relations with brother Dennis (resulting in a flurry of additional lawsuits). In the producer's chair was young, hip, 22-year-old Godfrey Diamond, newly minted and eager to please. A new band was in place as well; this lineup would form the beginning of what was to become known as 'The Everyman Band', and with a few more revolving members, they would remain with Lou to the close of the decade, very much to the advantage of the music.

There was a lot riding on the line. Despite the commercial successes of *Animal* and *Sally*, after *MMM*, Lou was heavily indebted to RCA. Label president Ken Glancy was a true believer, and he felt that with a strong new album, Lou could once again bounce back from commercial destitution just as he had done in the wake of the less-than-satisfactory showing of *Berlin*. As a result, Lou was committed, and while he was by no means sober, he displayed a strength of intention and control of the proceedings in the studio that had been missing. He allowed his players a distinct degree of unplanned and improvisatory input with regard to their parts, while simultaneously making very clear what was expected of the song itself. His ideas and instructions to Godfrey Diamond were both clear and detailed – nothing escaped his attention. Lou knew that it was sink-or-swim time, and this reality clearly helped with the sharpening of his focus, but was that the only catalyst at play here? The finished result shows that Lou was in a heightened state of inspiration for this album, and where that inspiration came from is central to not only the songs on this album but those of the next several albums, as well as our understanding of Lou Reed as the unique individual that he truly was.

As mentioned above, this album is a love letter, no question about it. The person these feelings were directed to is a central figure in the life and mythos of Lou Reed. Supposedly first seen as René De La Bush on the back cover of *Sally Can't Dance*, this person would become known as Rachel, the transgender individual that would be Lou's lover, companion, personal manager, and, it has been said, 'babysitter' for most of the mid to late 1970s. Born Richard Humphries, Rachel was a New York City afterhours denizen that frequented the bars and clubs of the city's underground populace, occasionally supporting herself through sex work and was more than capable of holding her own in a street fight, which, not only greatly impressed Lou but also saved his hide on a few occasions. Lou encountered Rachel at one of the many dark exclusive haunts he frequented in the midst of a multi-day drug binge, and as his oft-repeated account of their meeting indicates, she had no idea who he was, and when they left together and returned to his apartment, he babbled for hours about whatever, while she remained unimpressed, content to just wordlessly observe him as he ranted. Her lack of fawning adoration, let alone even tacit acknowledgment of Lou's star status, was very significant to him. Any study or analysis of celebrity shows a pattern similar to this: 'stars' seem to value and gravitate towards people who treat said star as an actual 'ordinary' person, as opposed to the mythical demigod consideration they seem to draw out of everyone they encounter, or the flurry of endless 'yes-people' they must professionally contend with. Lou's relationship with Rachel would influence his work unlike anything before, and some might say, since. Their union is gloriously celebrated in this soft, gentle album, and at the same time, the tumult of their subsequent breakup would fuel one of the greatest albums in Lou's discography a few years down the line.

Coney Island Baby was not quite the commercial success it was hoped for, but it did put Lou back into the public's gaze after the *Metal Machine Music* episode. It is an album that continues to divide listeners between those who value the lyrical and thematic content, and those who find the music sleepy, gentle and generally uninteresting. It is also important to bear in mind that all through the years and albums that have been discussed, as well as those yet to be discussed, Lou was constantly and relentlessly touring. He crisscrossed the US regularly, and his reputation in Europe was undiminished, largely due to both legend and regular continent-sweeping performance schedules. The release of *Coney Island Baby* would see no change in this activity; the album/tour/album/tour treadmill was essentially standard operating procedure for any successful recording artist of the era, and it would continue as such for years. Lou's many legal and contractual issues would finally come to a head at this time, with affairs escalating to the extent that he and Rachel would frequently be served papers as they would be leaving their apartment to go to work in the recording studio for both *Coney Island Baby* and the following LP. While Lou had been acting on his various resentments toward manager, record label, and anyone else that should happen to draw his ire, as a result of all of this combat, he was in dire financial straits. After the tepid showing of *Coney Island Baby*, RCA had about had it with his shit, too, yet with both parties at least in philosophical agreement to separate, where could Lou go next? With such a troublesome and erratic reputation, who might be willing to take the chance? Enter Clive Davis.

'Crazy Feeling' (Reed)

Strummy guitars with low-impact slide offer a soft landing to this first tune. Tried-and-true declarations of romantic yearnings fulfilled are on tap here, with uncomplicated language fitting the bill. Things do get a bit more interesting in the midst of the two sets of verses: 'And when I first seen you walk through that bar door/And I seen those suit-and-tie Johns buy you one drink/Then buy you some more', and then later on, 'Now everybody knows that business ends at three/And everybody knows an after-hours love is free', provide just a bit of a window into the nocturnal world where Lou met Rachel. Lou's deep appreciation of 'after-hours' haunts is well-documented. The chorus is a bright, sun-shiny blast of pep that ascends the heights of the 'Crazy Feeling' of love, richly augmented and celebrated by three-tonal glockenspiel peals to drive it all home. An easy, gentle, uncomplicated start to things.

'Charley's Girl' (Reed)

A four-square, thudding rhythm pushes things along while Bob Kulick distinguishes himself with colorful octave figures on guitar. Like the previous track, there is not much happening here, yet unlike the previous track, the lyrics don't add much to the Love Story on display. Apparently, somebody's girl, presumably Charley's, got the whole band in trouble, roll credits. The track is propulsive enough, with Michael Suchorsky giving added push with a tolling cowbell, which makes it a pleasant enough listen as is.

'She's My Best friend' (Reed)

Reaching back into the mists of the past, this VU chestnut is given a full mid-seventies, laid back and casual overhaul. The lyrics remain unchanged from 1968, which is unusual for a Lou retread. Bruce Yaw adds lift and dynamism with his opening high-register bass arpeggio, and the rest of the band drifts in. For a tale that testifies to a lover's uncanny ability to lift their partner out of misery, the chorus is most interesting:

If you want to see, see me, well baby, you know that I'm not around
But if you want to feel, feel me why don'tcha just turn around
I'm by the window where the light is

The band waxes and wanes throughout the track with cadence and crescendo appropriately. Of key interest is the fact that this is the first album since *Transformer* where Lou has picked up a guitar again, and the results are distinct. While lead duty is ably handled by Bob Kulick, with his tasteful and restrained voicings, the rhythm section, while fully competent in and of themselves, is enhanced by Lou's lock-step chordal chop ringing out true and clear. Lou *always* knew guitar players, and he always employed the very best, from Ronson to Hunter/Wagner, to Weis, and now Bob Kulick, who despite his understated performance here, was one of NYC's truly winning axe slingers. Rumor has it that he also responded to the same Village Voice ad that ultimately gave Ace Frehley his shot at stardom. Ironically, it was Bob's brother, Bruce Kulick, who spent the lion's share of the 1980s occupying the lead guitar chair for KISS. The familiar sound of Lou's driven strum is a welcome return to form, and to our benefit, it is now more or less here to remain.

'Kicks' (Reed)

On just about every Lou Reed album, there is always the outlier. It can save a flaccid, tepid album from total doldrums, and it can also jar the proceedings of a very fine album just enough to keep the listener on their toes. 'Kicks' is very definitely the *Coney Island Baby* outlier, to be sure, and what an outlier it is. Starting with the ambient sounds of a party in progress, complete with laughs and declarations, sounds of sharp edges tapping glass, and prolonged snorting noises that do not suggest the sticky dampness of seasonal allergies, the band falls in with a nervous, simmering groove that favors the ride cymbal. Lou and Bob Kulick's guitars are engaged in a perfect call-and-response dialog, and Lou weightlessly slips in and asks, shakily, desperately, 'Hey man, what's your style/How you get your kicks for livin'/Hey man, what's your style/How you get your adrenaline flowin' now'. What follows is a sweaty, jittery account of how the narrator greatly admires someone's ability to 'Get somebody to/to now come on to you and then/You kill them, You kill them/'Cause I need kicks/Hey baby babe I need kicks, now'. At 1:59, there is a jolt in volume that occurs between the lines 'When the blood come-a-down down his neck' ZAP! 'Don't you know that it was better than sex'. This audiological trick never fails to get a shock out of even the most casual listener. What started as a mid-party whisper, is ultimately kicked up to a full-tilt jaunt by the song's conclusion. It's a shame that this song was never a consideration for the soundtrack of William Friedkin's 1980 film *Cruising* as it would have been a perfect and thematically appropriate addition to the narrative.

'A Gift' (Reed)

Starting side two of the original LP, it's post-coital braggadocio time, and this song is it. Confidently crooning how he is 'a gift to the women of this world', the band provides a light, cloudlike track, complete with puffy, summer camp-like recorder notes to augment the melody. Apart from the wry, deeply tongue-in-cheek sentiment of the lyrics, which include such notable bon mots as 'Responsibility sits so ah hard on my shoulder/Like a good wine, I'm better as I grow older', and, crucially, 'It's hard to settle for second best/ After you've had me, you know you've had the best', this is not an especially interesting track, but the creepy atmospheric voices that repeat the song's title throughout add a needed dimension of weirdness.

'Ooohhh Baby' (Reed)

The attitude gets a bit more Lou-like on this track. Like most of the songs on this album, the sounds here are unobtrusive – the words are the main event. As we are shown, this is another late-night tete-a-tete betwixt the narrator and ... who? A date? An established romantic partner? A 'business associate'? Regardless, Lou seems to have a lot of information on this person: 'But now you're a topless dancer/working out of a bar on Times Square/And everybody wishes you were back/In the massage parlor back there on Ninth Avenue (311)'. Additionally:

> It's very funny asking me
> Why they keep the lights on down so low
> Well, yesterday's trade's today's competition
> Or didn't you know
> And all the fluorescent lighting makes it
> So your wrinkles, they don't show
> And it's very funny, the way your
> Twenty bucks an hour
> can a-go

Are these words John's lamentations toward an upwardly moving sex worker? Are they a Madam's consternation of a Lady who is growing too big for her britches? A suggested element of collage is once again suggested within the second set of verses: 'Your old man was the best B and E man/ Down on the streets/And all the guys on the precinct/Always was watching for him on their beat'.

As mentioned before, like many writers before and after him, Lou 'kept' characters. One of the many regular characters in his ever-changing living situations was someone described as the best breaking-and-entering criminal in the city. This person came from a very wealthy background; they committed crimes simply for the thrill they received from the process. Was this person the partner or father of the intention of the narrator's attention? Who knows, but this blending of tales makes for good content. Bob Kulick lays out a very Mick Taylor-esque slide solo in the middle of the song, and the rest of the band politely purrs along.

'Nobody's Business' (Reed)

Opening with sustained cymbal washes and loosely strummed chords, the song at first recalls 'Ocean', before Bruce Yaw signifies the song proper with a melodic bass introduction. As is once again befitting here, a low-wattage groove appears that allows Lou to suggest to a lover that it's time to chill and not rush things, while also refraining from easing off and allowing things to slide. The chorus consists of the song's title being repetitively stated, followed by a harmonized recitation of the word 'No' thirteen times. Nothing truly special here beyond that, to be sure.

'Coney Island Baby' (Reed)

The album's thematic centerpiece. Stretching out to six minutes and 46 seconds, this is the grand declaration of the glory of love that has been realized between Lou and Rachel. For an already musically low-key album, this song is the mellowest. The song begins as a two-chord murmur as Lou appears and brings us back to Freeport, LI, in the 1950s. Despite being weird, sexually fluid, and anxious, Lou 'wanted to play football for the coach'. Lou sing/speaks of his adolescent experience with a smooth calmness that serves the groove well.

Desiring and striving for a coach's admiration would seem to stand in direct opposition to his typical contrary position to such figures of traditional masculine strength and authority. Within this curious admission, a more substantial reckoning appears:

> 'Cause you know someday man you got to stand up straight
> Unless you're gonna fall
> And then you're goin' to die
> And the straightest dude I ever knew
> Was standing right by me all the time

Football may not just be football; the coach may be more than just the coach. After these sophomoric remembrances, a more substantial declaration appears:

> When you're all alone and lonely in your midnight hour
> And you find that your soul, it's been up for sale
> And you begin to think about all the things that you've done
> And begin to hate just about everything
> But remember the princess who lived on the hill
> Who loved you even though she knew you was wrong
> And right now she just might come shining through
> And the glory of love
> Glory of love
> Glory of love just might come through

The title of this song, as well as many of its lines and phrases, harken back once more to Lou's adolescence; specifically, his deep and passionate love of doo-wop, another trait he might be loathe to admit that he shares with Frank Zappa. The song's close is perhaps the sweetest and most doo-woppiest moment of the whole thing. As if presented by an old school DJ, this song has an on-air dedication: 'I'd like to send this one out to Lou and Rachel, and all the kids in PS 192/Man I swear I'd give the whole thing up for you'. This last line is stated just as the music recedes for the final time, and the effect on the listener is formidable. Dedicating the song to himself, his lover, and all the kids at his former Brooklyn elementary school is a very fine way to wind down this lover's tale of triumph against the odds of the world that they live in, and this is a couple, both in theory and practice, that faced strong odds. For an internationally renowned and celebrated popular culture artist to openly and unapologetically engage in and celebrate a non-heteronormative relationship in 1976 was unheard of. For decades upon decades, 'show business' had exerted and flexed Olympian degrees of energy and subterfuge with regard to 'covering' the non-traditional inclinations and orientations of their 'stars'. Knee-deep in the 21st century, lip service is paid to 'acceptance' and 'inclusiveness', but within the realms of our 'new realities' online, the same old hates and fears are roundly flexed and featured.

'Coney Island Baby' is a valid, vibrant call to notice of love's enduring and all-encompassing nature; stronger than hate, stronger than fear, stronger than bad luck. What Lou and Rachel discovered and shared is an irrefutable endorsement of the glory of love, concerning two people for whom life was not easy for any number of personal reasons. This song makes it real.

> When your two-bit friends have gone and ripped you off
> And they're talkin' behind your back sayin' man you are never
> Gonna be no human being
> Then you start thinkin' about all those things that you done
> And who it was and what it was
> And all the different things
> You made every scene
> But remember that the city is a funny place
> Something like a circus or a sewer
> And just remember different people have peculiar tastes
> And the glory of love
> The glory of love
> The glory of love
> Might see you through
> I'm a Coney Island Baby now

Feeling embarrassed, alienated, ashamed, isolated, stupid, foolish; all are cleansed and absolved by the glory of love. Lou and Rachel found something

Above: Lou finishes a cigarette. Pure rock 'n' roll, 1978. (*Rex Features*)

Left: The first self-titled solo LP, 1972. An unremarkable point of entry. (*RCA*)

Right: *Transformer*: The Watershed, 1972. A new lease on an artistic life, a lifeline to the disparate. (*RCA*)

Left: *Berlin*: The Magnum Opus that fell on deaf ears, 1973. (*RCA*)

Right: Let's rock (and make some coin) with *Rock 'n' Roll Animal*! 1974. (*RCA*)

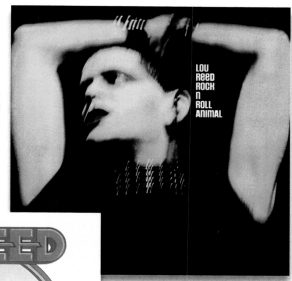

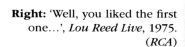

Left: Asleep at the wheel, the staff take over on *Sally Can't Dance*, 1974. (*RCA*)

Right: 'Well, you liked the first one…', *Lou Reed Live*, 1975. (*RCA*)

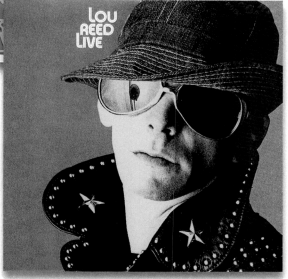

Above: Lou and his first wife, Bettye Kronstad, at their wedding party in 1973. Guess which one is drunk? (*Bettye Kronstad*)

Right: The Phantom of Rock spooks the kids, 1973. (*Gijsbert Hanekroot*)

Right: Mr. Jones and Mr. Reed look happy together, this time. 1973. (*Mick Rock*)

Below: Reed, Jagger and Bowie clearly enjoying the company of one another, 1973. (*Mick Rock*)

Above: A crop-haired demon issues directives, 1973. (*Getty Images*)

Below: Dick Wagner, Lou, Steve Hunter and temporary bassist, Peter Walsh, on stage in 1973. (*Gijsbert Hanekroot*)

Above: The Peroxide
Peril, touring for
Sally Can't Dance,
Paris in 1974.
(*Creative Common*)

Right: Lou
'shooting up'
onstage, a recurring
gimmick in 1974.
(*Mark Harmel*)

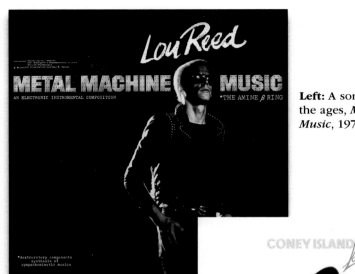

Left: A sonic iconoclast for the ages, *Metal Machine Music*, 1975. (*RCA*)

Right: *Coney Island Baby*: a musical love letter, and not the last, 1975. (*RCA*)

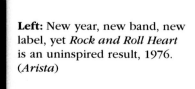

Left: New year, new band, new label, yet *Rock and Roll Heart* is an uninspired result, 1976. (*Arista*)

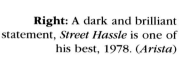

Right: A dark and brilliant statement, *Street Hassle* is one of his best, 1978. (*Arista*)

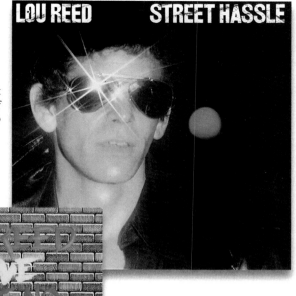

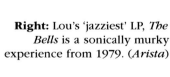

Left: *Take No Prisoners* is Lou's own 'Live in Vegas'. An inebriated rock 'n' roll *tour de force*, 1978. (*Arista*)

Right: Lou's 'jazziest' LP, *The Bells* is a sonically murky experience from 1979. (*Arista*)

Above: Lou taking care of business for a radio interview in 1975. (*Janet Macoska/ courtesy of Rock Paper Photo*)

Below: Cale, Lou and Warhol reminisce, NYC, 1976. (*Bob Gruen*)

Right: Lou and Rachel, his partner for many of his wildest years, in 1977. (*Jill Furmanovsky*)

Below: A pensive Lou bidding farewell to his reckless ways on stage, 1980. (*Michael Grecco*)

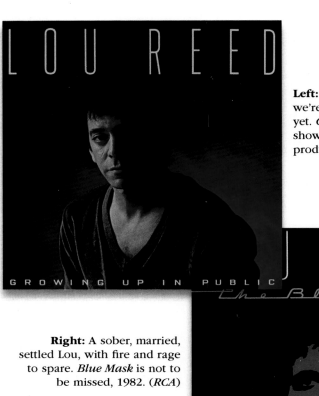

Left: Change is afoot, but we're not out of the woods yet. *Growing Up In Public* showcases crisp, florid production, 1980. (*Arista*)

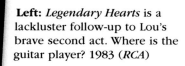

Right: A sober, married, settled Lou, with fire and rage to spare. *Blue Mask* is not to be missed, 1982. (*RCA*)

Left: *Legendary Hearts* is a lackluster follow-up to Lou's brave second act. Where is the guitar player? 1983 (*RCA*)

Right: The sober band tears up Italy on *Live In Italy* with blistering performances, 1984. (*RCA*)

Left: The 1980s are calling on 1984's *New Sensations*. (*RCA*)

Right: The 1980s are calling even louder on 1986's *Mistrial*. (*RCA*)

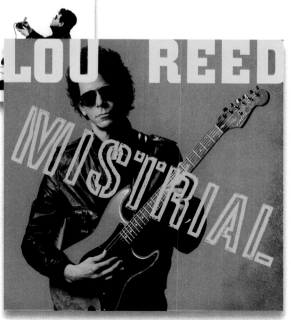

Above: Lou and Robert Quine making guitars do what they are supposed to do, 1984. (*Ebet Roberts*)

Below: Lou, Fernando Saunders and Quine on stage in Italy, 1984. (*Luciano Viti/Getty Images*)

Above: Saunders, Lou, Fred Maher and Quine in Italy, 1984. (*Luciano Viti/Getty Images*)

Below: Lou and Quine in Italy, 1984. 'My strat's better than *your* strat!' (*Luciano Viti/Getty Images*)

Left: The legendary Bataclan show in Paris, each player at the edge of becoming, 1972.

Right: *I'm So Free: The 1971 RCA Demos*: the quickly withdrawn origin story, 2021. (*RCA*)

Left: *Words and Music*: the lavishly packaged archive gem of a seed's germination, 2022. (*Light In The Attic*)

very special, and while it would not last, not unlike so many varieties of love, it was very, very real while it was here, and it is shared fully and thoroughly in this song.

Bonus Tracks
Unlike the majority of what are rolled out as bonus tracks on CD reissues, the *Coney Island Baby* bonus tracks are of great interest both historically and sonically. Of the six tracks on offer here, four are from the aborted January 1975 sessions for the album at Electric Lady studios in New York, and they feature Bob Meday on drums, Michael Fonfara on keyboards, and returning prodigal son Doug Yule on bass. The remaining two tracks are outtakes from the sessions proper at Mediasound studios from Autumn, 1975 and they feature the lineup as heard on the LP. The Electric Lady tracks are a fascinating listen. The music that would eventually become *Coney Island Baby* is most definitely the softer side of Lou, perhaps even verging on folk-rock, perish the thought. The initial, ultimately aborted recordings for the album from January are anything but.

'Downtown Dirt' (Reed)
There is a feral, teeth-gnashing rage ever present in the lyrics, the vocals themselves, and the band's performances. While never rising above a cold-blooded murmur, 'Downtown Dirt' lays out its disdain with no ambivalence.

> Pickin' up pieces of information
> down on the docks
> pickin' up pieces of information about you
> and how to pick locks
> Scoutin' around on the Lower East Side
> and mattresses in the rain
> Those uptown ladies with their uptown coats
> come down here to get laid
> It's a boring macho trip
> and I'm the type that fascinates

We are riding along as Lou's traveling partner in the nocturnal realms of urban vice once again. In the second set of verses, the invective becomes a bit more direct with the mention of a Miss Pamela Brown who lives in the Dakota; she is apparently 28 years old, has had a facelift, yet 'still looks so much older/Your bed is soiled/your linen is drab/You've got crabs'. The narrator provides this woman with the things she seems to need; credit cards are mentioned, as well 'I sell you sugar/I'm a humanitarian/I give it all to myself/That way your clean/And I stay addited(?)'. This is a curious lyrical inclusion; Lou has often stated that in his post-Pickwick Records, pre-VU days, he often sold drugs as a means of having money but mostly to keep him in personal supply. He would often sell his unsuspecting marks powdered sugar and keep the dope for himself, all the while being considerate enough to wait around and see if his customer would go into diabetic shock. He finishes things off by declaring, 'And psychologically y'know/Hey, psychologically it's better/ah that I think that I am dirt'. Between verses, Doug Yule and Bob Kulick engage in a slightly staggered two-note phrase that almost approaches jazz.

'Downtown Dirt' would see its final realization a few years later on the *Street Hassle* LP in a radically different format.

'Crazy Feeling' (Reed)
The three other Electric Lady tracks would see their full completion on the finished LP at the top of the following year. 'Crazy Feeling' maintains the same strummy, laid-back groove of the LP version, while a thoroughly pumped-up and hoarse-voiced Lou gives the vocals all he's got. The lyrics and story are largely unchanged.

'She's My Best Friend' (Reed)
This track is something to behold. The lyrics remain as they have always been, but the arrangement has been revved up to mimic Mott the Hoople at their most theatrical. Roaring, distorted guitars lay a rugged foundation for Michael Fonfara's strident and striding piano chords, while Lou tells us all about it with enthusiasm.

'Coney Island Baby' (Reed)
This track is here in true demo form, and while one can easily hear the elements in place that would become the penultimate final version, this has a casual, tentative air to it that shows a band at work, learning the licks. It starts with Lou strumming away on acoustic guitar while cajoling his bandmates into action with a 'C'mon, man!' Despite being a demo recording, there would seem to be overdubs here, as there is Lou's guitar, bass guitar, a second electric rhythm guitar, credited to Doug Yule, and Bob Kulick's curious controlled feedback tones that add a very unique lead guitar dynamic to the proceedings. The narrative and lyrics are generally the same as the final album version; it is atmosphere and emotion that go through major changes in order to bring us the full potential of the song in its final version.

'Nowhere At All' (Reed)
The remaining two bonus tracks come from the Media sound sessions that were responsible for the finished LP. The first of these, 'Nowhere at All', is a low-down super-greasy NYC rocker that is wholly incongruent with the songs that made the LP's final cut. Fuzzy guitars and funky drums move it along very well, with Bob Kulick squeezing off all kinds of brief but florid guitar God licks, and Bruce Yaw popping in at the high end of the register after

each chorus. The lyrics are an unremarkable mention of how the narrator is 'Nowhere at All' among the various challenging and troublesome people they might casually encounter. The main item here is the rough and ready groove of the track.

'Leave Me Alone' (Reed)

This is very similar to 'Nowhere at All', almost uncannily so, as they are even in the same key. 'Leave Me Alone' bears some similarity to its completed version on the upcoming *Street Hassle* LP, but this version lacks a certain degree of world-weary disgust and revulsion that makes the official version so complete. This demo version does contain some first draft lyrics; we hear about Lorraine, another botched facelift victim, and Lou even flirts with the limits of good taste (yet again) with some clever wordplay: 'I don't think I like the the the things that you do/I don't want to get ethnic, but I know that you're... through'. One can only imagine what else he might have used to complete that rhyme. Despite these slight alterations, the overall message of the song stands firm and unchanging.

Rock and Roll Heart (1976)

Personnel:
Lou Reed: vocals, guitar, piano
Marty Fogel: saxophone
Michael Fonfara: piano, Hammond organ, clavinet, ARP, synthesizer
Bruce Yaw: bass guitar
Michael Suchorsky: drums
Garland Jeffreys: backing vocals on 'You Wear it So Well'
Produced at: The Record Plant, NYC, by Lou Reed
Engineer: Corky Stasiak
Release Date: October 1976
Running Time: 37:42
Highest Chart Places: US: 64, UK: did not chart

New things are afoot: a new label, a new manager, a new lease on life. Clive Davis, the suave and sophisticated founder of Arista Records, had thrown Lou a lifeline of sorts. As the president of Columbia Records, Davis oversaw the acquisition and nurturing of countless new and subsequently sustained talents, as well as nourishing and furthering the careers of long-standing label stalwarts. Now at the helm of his own artist-forward label, he was interested in signing up-and-coming artists from the all-new, all-different 'punk' world, such as Patti Smith, and was also interested in fostering 'legacy' acts, such as Dionne Warwick. Lou would have a foot in both camps; as punk was rapidly distinguishing itself as the next new thing that the kids enjoy, he maintained the awkward position of both progenitor and participant. As a 'legacy' artist, he had the cumbersome history of the VU forever affixed to his name, plus the unpredictable, yet significant show of one or two hits from his solo career; perhaps he would rise again to reclaim commercial significance, as 'legacy' artists are by definition required to do.

How this meeting of the corporate and artistic minds came about is unclear. In Anthony DeCurtis' biography *Lou Reed: A Life*, the question of who reached out to who is unresolved. Lou is quoted as saying:

> There was just me and Rachel ... living at the fucking Gramercy Park Hotel on fifteen dollars a day, while lawyers are trying to figure out what to do with me. Then I get a call from Clive Davis ... and he said, 'Hey, how ya doing? Haven't seen you for a while'. He knew how I was doing. He said, 'Why don't we have lunch?' I felt like saying, 'You mean you want to be seen with me in public?' If Clive could be seen with me, I had turned a corner. I grabbed Rachel and said, 'Do you know who just called?' I knew then that I'd won.

The idea of 'winning' against his adversaries is crucial to Lou's perception of this turn of events. Conversely, Clive Davis has himself gone on record claiming that it was in fact, Lou that reached out to him, begging for aesthetically like-minded assistance from his perilous circumstances. Regardless, Lou was now freed from RCA's roster and was now an Arista artist. At the same time, Lou had a new manager in Johnny Podell. As manager of the careers and tours of Alice Cooper, The Allman Brothers and Crosby, Stills, Nash, and Young, among others, looking after the affairs of Lou for the next year did not offer any great additional professional prestige, but Podell's freebase habit dovetailed nicely with Lou's speed habit, and Podell and his wife Monica, a popular Manhattan model at the time, along with Lou and Rachel, were a very 'now' double-date quartet on the town.

As for the music, once again, much was on the line. Would Davis' investment pay off? As much as a believer in the vision and integrity of the artist as his reputation beheld, he was also very much a shrewd and canny businessman, and never the twain shall meet. The musicians involved had not changed dramatically from the last LP. One new presence is sax player Marty Fogle, the final brick in the Everyman Band façade, and his musical presence would from here on greatly add to Lou's music for the duration of the decade. Michael Fonfara is rightly returned to his position of keyboardist and bandleader, but the guitar chair is occupied by Lou alone. Having 'had' to fire Bob Kulick for the unpardonable sin of rehearsing new material with the band before they could be properly instructed by Lou, his fate was sealed. As a result, the songs are keyboard and brass-heavy, with a fulsome rhythm section holding it down expertly. The songs, however, were another matter.

The unfortunate reality here is that, like *Lou Reed* from four years previous, *Rock and Roll Heart* is ultimately poor stuff. This fact is especially glaring given all that was at stake. As far as the youthful concerns of 'punk rock' were concerned, the general easy-listening vibe can in no way suggest or even acknowledge its presence. As for how a stronger connection to a more 'adult' audience might be concerned, the basic, contrived exercises in narrative simplicity, as well as the musical banality, with most songs struggling to last for more than two minutes, will leave ageing 30-somethings, a cohort to which Lou was most certainly a member, bored and unenthused. This was an especially sour fact when considering all the new opportunities Lou had been afforded. Given the greater trajectory of his career, this is not atypical, but an album this ordinary was little more than another artistic misstep. Fortunately for us, the moon waxes and wanes, and the tides rush in and out, both containing a reliable yet mercurial process.

'I Believe in Love' (Reed)
This bright, sunny, peppy, upbeat number is our starting point, and if not for Lou's wobbly, barely on-key vocal, this would be a perfect demo for The Carpenters. This is an odd, low-impact opening statement for the OG New York City rock 'n' roll poet at the height of the punk rock era, occurring at a time of managerial and record label revision, as well as, hopefully,

commercial rebirth. Clive Davis apparently felt that this song had single potential if only Lou would consent to additional sweetening in the studio. To no one's great surprise, Lou refused, and Davis even went so far as to appeal to Michael Fonfara, the band leader, to see if he could talk some sense into his boss. No dice. Lyrically, little is on offer here, just pallid announcements on the belief of music, good times, love, etc. Sadly, this would set the standard for most of the LP's duration.

'Banging on My Drum' (Reed)

'I'm banging on my drum/I'm having lots of fun' is basically all that is on offer here, word-wise. What does this mean? Is this a celebration of individuality? Independence? Masturbation? Doin' your own thing, man? Actually playing the drums? As per usual, it's up to us to decide. The music ups the pulse rate a bit with a basic Chuck Berry riff, and the song ends with Lou rolling through some garden variety Chuck Berry, Keith Richards, Johnny Thunders riffs, before the song closes with what must be one of the most abrupt and jarring fade-outs in music history. Two minutes and twelve seconds of arbitrary drum-banging.

'Follow the Leader' (Reed)

Until the 2001 release of *The Quine Tapes*, the fact that this was another revisited VU relic was unknown. Sadly, that seventeen-minute-plus version, despite the poor sound quality, is the better version. Here, Michael Suchorsky earns overtime pay with a busy propulsive rhythm that is aided and assisted with percussion overdubs. Marty Fogle honks and squawks with authority, while Michael Fonfara decorates the groove with active clavinet. Then there's Lou. Once again, the lyrics are sparse. We are advised to follow the leader, work up a sweat if we want to dance, and if time allows, find a better romance, all in New York City. The key difference here is delivery. Lou spits and stutters his syllables as only he can, turning a somewhat banal syntactical reading into a true vocal performance as if his tongue and vocal cords are just another percussive component to the thick stew of the beat. Yet another track that barely cracks the two-minute barrier.

'You Wear it So Well' (Reed)

Things get a bit more substantial here. The track is shadowy and dark, driven by Fonfara's piano, and there is enough reverb to summon ghosts. Lou's old Syracuse buddy Garland Jeffreys, who by this point was a distinguished singer/songwriter on his own, joins in on background vocals. What follows is a gentle, loving tribute to the many ills and stresses a person must bear each day, as seen through the eyes of their lover:

All those things yeah that you've got to give
yeah you wear it so well

And all of those stories honey that I know you could tell
yeah you wear it so well
And your face hides it so I can't tell
That you knew it so well... All of the things that made the poets sing
You wear it so well, yeah, you hide it so well
And all of the pain that you used to tell
You hide it so well... Grace and style
Equals you so well

To be truly seen for the whole person we really are, and to be accepted as such by whom we are fortunate enough to be able to consider our partner, is a rare and sacred joy. A key aspect of this interpersonal dynamic is to see and recognize the many masks and guises one must wear as a means of acknowledging and accomplishing each given day's events. This is something each and every one of us is required to do, simply as a means of paying the cost of being alive. If we are fortunate enough to find another person with whom we can share the burden of existence, for that person to not only regularly see behind our masks but also accept and love what lies beneath, makes the universe just a little bit less of such a dark, vast, uncaring place. More directly, looking at this song's ideas as a series of statements that Lou might make to Rachel throws the ideas of the glory of love once again into high relief. Rachel never got to tell her story as neither Rachel nor Ricky; she never got to remove any of the many masks that she must have had to cling to and reinforce in her life. Her partner recognizes that while she is here, beneath whatever pain and anger that might exist, she wears those masks very well, with élan and aplomb, and survives and succeeds in spite of it all.

'Ladies Pay' (Reed)

This minor chord song gives attention to the burden a woman must endure when her wayfaring lover is errant: 'The poor sick soldier lies in bed beside his girl/Thinking of another place on the other side of this world/Ah how the ladies pay/when the men they have has gone away'. The key significance here is that this is the most guitar-forward track on the album. Lou etches out raw, drawling, feedback-laden scrawls that are curiously restrained in the mix, yet they make up the majority of the song's four minutes and 23-second duration, nearly double the time of most of the LP's tracks.

'Rock and Roll Heart' (Reed)

The title track. Starting with roaring power chords, this simple song goes on to list the many things the narrator does not like, such as opera, ballet, New Wave French movies, messages or 'something to say', and resolves things with 'I guess that I'm dumb 'cause I know I ain't smart/But deep down inside I've got a rock and roll heart'. In spite of all of this, the song has a very durable, singable chorus where the song's title is repeated over a bed of simple chords. As a result, the song has a hidden lasting quality; you might find yourself humming and mumbling the chorus at odd times of your day, in spite of yourself.

'Chooser and the Chosen One' (Reed)
Beginning side two of the LP, we have ... an instrumental? This is a very distinct oddity for a Lou Reed album, and it smacks of filler. The first 40 seconds feature Marty Fogle in full flight with something that would not be out of place on ECM records. What follows is a gentle hippy jam that recalls The Grateful Dead at their most polished. As far as the legacy of Lou Reed is concerned, this is two minutes and 46 seconds of 'Huh?'

'Senselessly Cruel' (Reed)
Marty Fogle guides us through the simple melody and bouncy rhythm before Lou rolls back the hands of time in a deadpan revisitation of, presumably, the first girl who broke his heart:

> But now the time has come to lay waste
> The theory people have of getting an acquired taste
> You treated me oh so so senselessly cruel

There is truly nothing else going on here, and the song crosses the finish line at just barely over two minutes.

'Claim to Fame' (Reed)
The adventures in MOR continue unabated with yet another pale exercise. The band, the music, the production, the vocals, the lyrics; all are unexceptional, as is sadly the case with most of this album. The lyrics rattle off a list of descriptions that seem to challenge someone's ability to 'make it' independently, questioning this person's 'claim to fame'. We can leave it at that.

'Vicious Circle' (Reed)
The vibe is switched up just a bit here with a gentle acoustic guitar intro and bass duties handled by Michael Fonfara on a heavily phased electric piano. It's a much mellower mood here, and it serves the lyrics well. Never once rising above a baritone croak, Lou speaks of the 365 degrees of cross-current influence that is often wielded by those we are the closest to. These people are described as our 'so-called friends':

> Cause some people think that they like problems
> And some people think that they don't
> And for everybody who says yes
> There's somebody whose starin' sayin' don't

Lou can be forgiven here for rhyming 'don't' with 'don't' – it applies to the narrative. At the close of the tune, 'surrounded by your so-called friends' has been curiously altered to 'surrounded by all your friends'. This alteration can seem subtle or distinct, depending on the listener and their circumstances.

'A Sheltered Life' (Reed)

Originally appearing as a rough 1967 demo on the *Peel Slowly and See* box set, this version is given the full jazzbo, hepcat, bop combo treatment, with appropriately walking bass, authoritative sax, and meandering flute. Lou reels off an obviously fictional list of things he has never done, such as a tongue-firmly-planted-in-cheek admission of 'I've never taken dope/I've never taken drugs/I've never danced on a bear skin rug'. This is clearly and obviously a character study, as opposed to a self-referential study. Lou's vocal revels in its jaded, world-weary tone that perfectly suits the words, while Marty Fogle's competing overdubbed reeds give this track its jazz credentials as the song fades out effortlessly. Lightweight costume fun for a lightweight album.

'Temporary Thing' (Reed)

At the end of the album, we come to the outlier. As previously mentioned, the outlier can lift a lacking album out of the depths and into illumination. With this album, the outlier has an especially heavy burden due to the general mediocrity of the LP's sum total. 'Temporary Thing' primarily stands out because of its uncut purity. The watered-down gentility that coats most of this album has been stripped away here, as band, singer, and lyrics reveal strained, bared teeth in their intent and delivery. Any song that commences with 'Hey now bitch', might very well indicate that a bumpy ride is in store. Beginning with a strong declarative drum-and-piano stomp, Michael Suchorsky rigorously counts out fours on the high hat. The tale within is little more than a lover's spat; it's the gritty intensity of the performative declarations, both musical and lyrical, that make the difference:

You read too many books, you seen too many plays
And if things like this turn you away
Now look, hey look you'd better think about it twice
I know that your good breeding makes it seem not so nice
It's just a temporary thing... Where's the number, where's the dime and where's the phone
I feel like a stranger, I guess you're gonna go back home
Your mother, your father, your fucking brother
I guess they wouldn't agree with me
But I don't give two shits
They're no better than me
Uh huh
It's just a temporary thing

This is a sad, yet perhaps typical moment amongst lovers; as much as we hate to admit it, moments like these do happen in relationships, and they are neither pretty nor healthy. What exists here is a very real, very human expression of ugliness. The band hangs on Lou's every murmur and spurt, infinitely in tune with their singer's performance and intent. Each of the many ups and downs that might happen between us, it's just a temporary thing, so why don't you just chill, or get out of here, or shut the fuck up, because this, too, will pass. Ugly, ugly sentiments, but they are just another part of the thorough payload of real love. This visceral, stinging exposition is a musical success in and of itself – the album's only truly worthwhile track.

Street Hassle (1978)

Personnel:
Lou Reed: guitar, bass guitar, piano, vocals
Stuart Heinrich: guitar in 'Street Hassle,' backing vocals on 'Leave Me Alone'
Michael Fonfara: piano on 'I Wanna be Black' and 'Shooting Star'
Marty Fogle: saxophone
Steve Friedman: bass guitar on 'Leave Me Alone'
Jeffrey Ross: lead guitar, backing vocals on live tracks
Michael Suchorsky: drums
Aram Schefrin: string arrangement
Genya Ravan: backing vocals
Jo'Anna Kameron: backing vocals
Angela Howard: backing vocals
Christine Wiltshire: backing vocals
Bruce Springsteen: backing vocals on 'Street Hassle: Slipaway'
Produced at: Record Plant Studios, NYC, by Lou Reed and Richard Robinson
Engineer: Rod O'Brien
Engineers of live recordings: Manfred Schunke and Heiner Friesz
Assistant Engineers: Gray Russell and Tony Caruso
Release Date: February 1978
Running time: 36:15
Highest Chart Places: US: 89, UK: did not chart

After the completion of *Rock and Roll Heart*, manager Johnny Podell
convinced Arista to finance a tour. This jaunt would see Lou and his band
flanked on stage by a wall of flickering, semi-functional televisions that
Lou, photographer Mick Rock, who was responsible for a series of Lou's
album covers at this time, and young, new guitarist Jeffrey Ross had scooped
up off the streets and out of the gutters. The result was distracting but
effective. During this tour, of both the US and Europe, Lou's behavior began
to degenerate in ways that started to push the envelope too far. There
were frequent instances of knives being pulled on journalists and record
executives, and Lou's speed intake – at times administered via eyedrops –
reached towering heights, creating a paranoid, irascible, unpredictable person
that was difficult to work with, let alone be around. His relationship with
Rachel bore the ups and downs of any romantic connection, but all observant
parties involved agreed that Lou and Rachel were the light in each other's
lives. At the start of the European leg of the tour, they celebrated their three-
year anniversary in grand style with a three-tiered cake at Maunkberry's, a
gay club in London. The event was photographed for *Rock Scene* magazine,
and later in the year, Mick Rock produced color photos of the couple for
a five-page spread to coincide with an interview with Victor Bockris in the
pornographic magazine *National Screw*. Remember, this is 1977. For a pop
star to even be associated with pornography in any way was a sure-fire

career ender (unless, of course, you were Andrea True). To proudly appear in a pornographic publication with your non-binary partner of three years is iconoclastic. On this European tour, Rachel's role expanded to manager, minder, do-er, and getter. Despite this, the eventual gradual unraveling of their relationship would be the fuel and fire of *Street Hassle*, one of the greatest albums of Lou's career.

For Johnny Podell, he would be shown the door after making the mistake of introducing Lou to lawyer Eric Kronfeld. For his trouble, Kronfeld was promptly installed as Lou's manager and would serve that role into the 1980s. Kronfeld oversaw Lou settling with Steve Katz but poured gas on the fire for the ongoing litigation with Dennis Katz, resulting in Lou giving evidence at the Supreme Court of New York State. Despite less-than-stellar record sales, touring continued to be lucrative, and the European tour of 1977 would yield results that would find their way onto the next album. Initially, Lou wanted to release these live recordings untouched, but Arista made clear that another live LP was out of the question. Live tracks did end up coming out but in augmented form. Lou, ever the techie, had become fascinated with a method of recording that attempted to perfectly reproduce the stereoscopic experience as processed by the two ears on either side of the human head. Called Binaural Sound, it was developed by German sound engineer Manfred Schunke, and it involved two microphones placed on either side of a Styrofoam dummy head in the studio or performance space. While interesting in theory, it left a bit to be desired in practice; if the listener was not listening through headphones, the effect was lost, and the album that he and reunited first album producer Richard Robinson created ended up sounding a bit weird. Despite this, Lou found the approach fascinating, and he used it for his next three albums, including a two-LP live set.

Schunke was on hand to record a handful of live dates on this tour, including a show in Germany that would see an unofficial release, which Lou would then manipulate and overdub in the studio to create a live/studio collage. As a result, Lou came up with one of his most sonically unique albums, after *Metal Machine Music*, of course. As mentioned above, this LP reveals Lou's navigation through the dissolution and aftermath of his and Rachel's breakup. The music contained herein is some of the ugliest, angriest, funniest, most desperate, and – of highest significance – the most human work of Lou's canon.

To no one's great shock, the album was, once again, a chore to make; Bruce Yaw ended up leaving Lou's employment as a result of financial issues, and Richard Robinson walked out mid-session after an argument with Lou, not to return. Lou's drink and drug use continued at full force throughout. Despite this, critics were almost universally magnanimous in their spirited praise and celebration of the LP upon release – it was celebrated almost as a return of the prodigal child. After years of what seemed (to them) like so much piddling bullshit, Lou was *back*. Nice ideas, to be sure, but as we all know, praise does not 'shift units', as the industry parlance goes, and without any kind of single to send out to radio, the new Lou Reed LP quickly sank in sales once again. Lou was, once more, angry, but he was not finished here; he had more to say on the various subjects within, and he wanted his 'live' Binaural Sound LP as well. He, and we, would get such a beast in the form of his next release, a double-live LP recorded at The Bottom Line in NYC in May 1978 at the end of the *Street Hassle* tour. What a live document it is!

'Gimmie Some Good Times' (Reed)

Starting off with a deliberately image-puncturing dialog, Lou gives himself shit to the tune of a very familiar chord progression. Lou #1 and Lou #2 are divided by Lou #1's contribution presented with a #1 in front of it, while Lou #2 has a #2 in the same place in the following transcript:

1) Hey, if it ain't the Rock 'n' Roll Animal himself, What you doin', bro?
2) Standin' on the corner
1) Well I can see that. What you got in your hand?
2) Suitcase in my hand
1) No shit! What it is!
2) Jack is in his corset, Jane is in her vest
1) Fuckin' faggot junkie
2) Sweet Jane, I'm in a rock and roll band
1) Well, I can see that

As we can see, Lou #2 is merely quoting 'Sweet Jane'. This is the opening on Lou's first album since punk had been elevated to the cultural touchstone that it would remain. Despite being revered as a punk godfather of sorts, he was never comfortable with this designation, and being the lifelong contrarian that he was, the slaughtering of this particular sacred cow seemed pertinent. Basing such a desecration against the chords of one of his most memorable songs only drives the point home that much stronger. Lyrically, there is not much else beyond the song's title to bank on. The chorus: 'Gimmie, gimmie, gimmie some good times/Gimmie, gimmie, gimmie some pain/No matter how ugly you are/you know to me it all looks the same'. The LP's overall sound and tone are also introduced here, and they are a curiosity, as the mix seems clouded by a midrange-centered blur. The live/studio sonic collage is not a new concept here; The Grateful Dead's *Anthem of the Sun*, Blue Cheer's *Outside Inside,* and many recordings by Frank Zappa, among countless others, all share the same concept, yet the results are all unique in their own ways. With *Street Hassle*, the auditory distinction between live and studio is not easily detectable beyond quickly faded spurts of applause at the close of some songs. The mix here and throughout the LP has a grimy, grainy glisten to it that suggests substantial after-the-thought tinkering. On this track, Lou sings the chorus section in a heady wash of wavering harmony voices; a novel and effective effect given the recording's heavy-handed sonic pedigree.

'Dirt' (Reed)

The filter, any kind of filter, is removed and discarded here. While this song, in rough form, had been in the vaults for a bit of time, this definitive version is known to be inspired by and dedicated to former manager Dennis Katz, with whom Lou was involved in rich and protracted litigation. The song here is compromised in the extreme; it begins with a distracted guitar that is brought in by scrubby tape noises, throbbing, loud bass, another seemingly unrelated guitar, and sustained piano chords before Lou's booming voice comes in with an odd, chorus-effected speak/sing vocal which lays down the law of his intentions. The track continues to barely keep from musically falling apart for its 4:46 duration, and after the relative polish of the LP's first track, it sets the stage once again for the avant-garde vs. ineptitude artistic gestalt of the album that can only be conclusively decided by each listener independently. The lyrics revel in unvarnished spite:

> You're a pig of a person, there's a justice in this world
> Hey, how about that? ...
> You and people like you
> That no principle has touched, no principles baptized
> How about that?
> Who'd eat shit and say it tasted good
> if there was some money in it for 'em... You're just dirt

Late Texas musician Bobby Fuller gets a name check amongst the proceedings in a reference that is not abundantly clear. Lou quoting 'I fought the law and the law won', could be seen as Lou casting himself as the law, and his victim, Dennis Katz, as the one who fights the law and loses. Again, the music must be addressed here. The guitars sound confused and hesitant, often conflicting with each other as a third guitar joins the proceedings. After the third verse, the drums begin a heavily gated tribal thud that offers little foundation. At 1:24, the bass attempts a thoroughly shaky and unsure chord change, while the drums try to follow, which almost grounds the whole thing, however, the track's overall weightlessness renders it from ever being totally grounded. This is not failure or ineptitude on the artist's part; it in fact, adds greatly to the lyrical mood of utter disgust and revulsion. At 3:50, the background vocalists join in to harmonize on 'Cheap, cheap, cheap, cheap, uptown dirt', before things grind down at 4:37 to the quickly faded sound of an applauding audience. It is a challenge to imagine this song coming off on stage as is, which once again blurs the division between the live/studio distinction of each song on the LP.

'Street Hassle' (Reed)

The centerpiece, and not merely by name. This track stands out as one of the very pillars of Lou's output, both musically and lyrically. This eleven-minute, all-done-in-the-studio track is divided into three titled sections and has been interpreted as Lou's very real and unshielded response to the dissolution of his relationship with Rachel.

'Waltzing Matilda'

Starting with a spritely cello trio, the lift and lightness of the figure played in no way betray the emotional intensity to come. Keyboard and rhythm guitar float in, and we are told of a union between Waltzing Matilda and the unnamed Sexy Boy. It has been suggested that Matilda is a transgendered person, and while Lou has said that the relevance of pronouns in his lyrics is significant, this discloses and also obscures nothing. Matilda and the Sexy Boy are negotiating the terms of their imminent connection:

> Waltzing Matilda whipped out her wallet
> The sexy boy smiled in dismay
> She took out four twenties 'cause she liked round figures
> Everybody's queen for a day
> Oh babe, I'm on fire and you know I admire your body
> Why don't we slip away
> Although I'm sure you're certain it's a rarity me flirtin'
> Sha-la-la-la this way

The 'Sha-la-la-las' that make their way into the lyrics serve many possible functions here. They can be seen as a harkening back to Lou's adolescent love of doo-wop. They can be seen as a term of art the writer uses to perhaps politely obscure some of the more tender physical moments and movements between the two characters on display. And they can be seen as a dada-like verbal stand-in to cover the mild awkwardness between two relative strangers and/or future lovers that undoubtedly pops up at times like these in any circumstance. What is most clear about this song is what is also most significant. This is an experience between a sex worker and their 'John'. As we see in the second set of verses, their union is far from tawdry, dangerous, or cheap, as such an experience is often very stereotypically portrayed.

> And then sha-la-la-la-la he entered her slowly and showed her where he was coming from
> And then sha-la-la-la-la he made love to her gently it was like she never ever come
> And then sha-la-la-la-la, sha-la-la-la-la
> When the sun rose and he made to leave
> You know sha-la-la-la-la, sha-la-la-la-la
> Neither one regretted a thing

This interlude concludes with no regret, no shame, and with the exception of 80 dollars, no sense of loss or sacrifice for either party. Lou sings with an earnestness and devotion to the subject matter throughout all three sections of the song, and it makes an invaluable difference. The first part ends with a final one-note string cadence to match the last gaze these parting lovers might share.

'Street Hassle'
Following the joys of the first part, things become sour here. This section begins with a plaintive unaccompanied voice of Genya Ravan lingering through a soft melody not unrelated to the song itself. It could be the sound of weeping, of drowning, of slipping away. The voice stops on an unintelligible syllable before the cello trio begins again; this time, each cello falls in independently, with the first of the three playing simple octave figures, the second joining with the melody, while the third fades in to double the melody. This concludes with the fade-in of a female chorus intoning 'Slipaway' while the cellos are replaced by guitars, and, finally, a voice. What follows is a cold and squalid monologue about how to dispose of the body of a recently deceased person as a consequence of an overdose.

> Hey that cunt's not breathing, I think she's had too much
> Of something or other, hey man, you know what I mean?
> I don't mean to scare you, but you're the one who came here
> And you're the one who's got to take her when you leave... Sha-la-la-la-la
> man, why don't you just slip her away

The words are delivered in a tone of simmered calculation; a slow burning pushiness that bares no illusions about the speaker being solely interested in their own safe passage from this difficult circumstance. The return of the 'sha-la-la-la-las' tries to add a measure of casualness to the otherwise catastrophic scene, as if it's just another day in the Big City. This idea is further explored in the second set of verses.

> It's either the best or it's the worst
> And since I don't have to choose, I guess I won't
> And I know this ain't no way to treat a guest
> But why don't you grab your old lady by the feet
> And just lay her out on the darkened street and by morning
> She's just another hit-and-run

The song concludes with some of Lou's finest lines. They transcend the characters and struggles on display in the 'Street Hassle' triptych; they speak to a life lived outside of most things that some, in fact, many people might never imagine missing or lacking. These can, of course, be material things, but what is mentioned here goes beyond possessions of the physical or the corporeal. Such an absence can lead to a terrible, fruitless searching that only results in greater loss and alienation.

You know some people got no choice
And they can never find a voice
To talk with
That they can even call their own
So the first thing that they see
That allows them the right to be
Why they follow it
You know it's called
Bad Luck

These are the people Lou was most interested in singing about; truly giving a voice to those crippled by their life's bad luck. Where this bad luck came from is anybody's guess. That does not really matter; it's the one true reality that people can see and cling to simply because it is their own, and Lou wants these people to have something else of their own as well. The section ends plainly with a brief pause before section three.

'Slipaway'

This third and final part begins with throbbing bass guitar mimicking the cello's octave figure. Piano floats in, followed by the return of the cellos, some random guitar riffs, and a snare drum, before all instruments stop, save the snare, and the guitars return to their riffs – and we then hear ... Bruce Springsteen? Apparently, he was in the room downstairs recording his fourth LP, *Darkness on the Edge of Town*, when Lou felt that a short spoken piece would be better suited to his voice rather than his own. What follows is a brief recitation of lines about a 'real song', a 'painful song', the kind that 'life is full of', all delivered in Springsteen's unmistakable early-career drawl that ends with a very tongue-in-cheek 'though tramps like us we were born to pay'. Following this, Lou gets back down to business with some remarkably emotional exorcising, sung in a wavering voice that bleeds with intention.

Love has gone away and there's no one here now and
There's nothing left to say but, oh how I miss him, baby
Ah baby, come on and slip away
Come on baby
Why don't you slip away
Love has gone away, took the rings off my fingers
And there's nothing left to say
But oh how, oh how I need it
Baby
Come on baby, I need you baby
Oh please don't slip away
I need your loving so bad Babe
Please don't slip away

Lou has never been the most gifted or colorful singer by a long shot, but his performance here leaves no doubt that this comes deeply from within, as the feeling just drips from his delivery. He has spoken about how Rachel actually did remove rings from his fingers in one of their final breakups; there can be little doubt as to whom the pronoun within refers to. The narrative switch from begging his departed lover to slip away, and then revisiting that idea by pleading with them not to, is a very simple yet astute look at the duality of emotions one can go through during a protracted breakup – it's a good idea, it's a bad idea; you'd better go, you'd better stay. 'Street Hassle' is one of Lou's greatest triumphs musically, lyrically, and artistically. It stands alone.

'I Wanna be Black' (Reed)
Ah, yes. *That* song. Starting off side two of the original LP is one of Lou's not only most controversial songs but also one he has actually tried to distance himself from over the years. The song begins with an authoritative boom that sonically exposes the song's live origins more clearly; this can be said for the majority of the tracks on side two. A bouncing, pseudo-RnB rhythm moves along competently, while odd, refracted overdubbed guitar lines scurry in and out of the mix. This, too, is indicative of the sound of the larger LP as a whole. The main event here, obviously, is the lyrics. Just what is this supposed to mean? Is this an attempt at fun with stereotypes? Is Lou racist? Is this parody, and if so, a parody of whom or what?

I wanna be black
Have natural rhythm
Shoot twenty feet of jism, too
And fuck up the jews... I wanna be black
I wanna be like Malcom X
And cast a hex over President Kennedy's tomb
And have a big prick, too

Whoops. It is on the chorus where intentions might become a bit clearer: 'I don't wanna be a fucked-up, middle-class college student no more'. Various biographers have mentioned this song's possible connection to some of the ideas in Norman Mailer's controversial and career-cementing essay *The White Negro* from 1957. Mailer addresses what he says is the birth of the 'hipster' in American culture; a youth figure who, traumatized by both nuclear weaponry and the, at the time, recent Holocaust in Europe, adapts certain modes of cultural and interpersonal attitudes and behaviors, both of which Mailer attributes to be appropriated from 'negro culture'. Twenty years later, in grossly simplified and diluted form, Lou revisits the idea of cultural adaptation when he sings, or his character in the song sings, about not wanting to be what he perceives himself to be anymore, and wishing to become something else that he has envisioned solely through the lens of a gross and degrading stereotype. With this having been said, is it still okay to sing this, with its utterly crucial reliance on the listener to not only see through the layers of stereotype but also to allow oneself to be 'in on the joke?' As mentioned above, this is one that Lou himself backed away from at various points in his career, and while never outright apologizing or explaining anything, his reticence is telling. With regard to any trace of actual humor at play here, it is pretty hilarious to hear Jo'Anna Kameron, Angela Howard, and Christine Wiltshire harmonize 'Fuck up the Jews', 'Have a big prick, too', and 'Fucked-up college student NO MORE!' after the second set of verses, if only for the sake of pure absurdity.

'Real Good Time Together' (Reed)
We would not know of this song's origins until its inclusion on the 1986 barrel-scraping VU compilation *Another View*, although Patti Smith had been opening her shows with this song for a few years by this point. The version here traverses the studio-to-live matrix, with its beginning laying down a blueprint for many of the neo-psyche bands that would pop up in the 1980s; Spacemen 3 especially comes to mind, as they would even feature their own 'Ode to Street Hassle' on their very fine second LP. Humming, undulating, vibrating guitars roll out of each side of the stereo, while Lou's booming, multi-tracked voice runs through variations of the song's title. After about two-thirds of the song, arrhythmic backing vocals bring the rest of the band towards a triumphant climax, driven by Michael Suchorsky's propulsive drums.

'Shooting Star' (Reed)
This song was apparently learned by the band on stage in Germany, and while there is no guarantee that this is that particular recording, this track begins with the clumsy footing of a toddler's first steps. One by one, each instrument falls into place to allow Lou the space to wax abstract. The lyrics are a curious blend of images and ideas:

All of the people had their share of the glory
Looking out after you
It's just a story about win, lose, or glory
And you know that it's true... Some man-made glory won't permit the commission
Of another God
And later persuasion would permit rearranging
Of another bar
And to cause more confusion and to make a dis-illusion
Would have gone too far
And it's by admission a protracted admission
A cadillac metallic car... Uh huh, oh yeah, you're just a shooting star

What is he exactly talking about here? The chorus, about the 'Shooting Star', can be seen as a comment on his predicament as an active participant in popular culture, but is that all that is going on here? The lines about 'man-made glory' not being able to 'permit the commission of another god' are most curious. Any broad measure of human expression would lead us to believe that the works of humans would seem to stand in constant and pale contrast to the efforts of the divine, yet if it is us who create our gods, where does this lyric leave us? How does this uncomplicated idea connect to what follows, ideas about 'later persuasion' not allowing a 'rearrangement' of 'another bar'? A bar of music? A bar where drinks are served? Is the designation of a certain standard to be raised or lowered? This could be a creative statement on the nature of songwriting; the questions of how an artist considers a work *finished*, and how the artist might negotiate potential sources of further inspiration after the fact. Then there is the mention of a 'Cadillac, metallic car'. With Lou, it is always possible that there is no stronger meaning here; he is merely playing with words and rhymes. As for the band, once they all come together, they maintain a hard stomp that is melodically held in place by Marty Fogle's sax. The track ends with a typical on-stage ending and quickly faded applause.

'Leave Me Alone' (Reed)

Getting an update from the *Coney Island Baby*-era demo, this track features overhauled lyrics, a key change, and most crucially, a slower tempo; this distinct alteration greatly serves the proceedings. The band provides a sludgy, grinding groove that sustains Lou's strained lamentation, wishing that the various sycophants and parasites in his life would just leave him alone. Once again, Marty Fogle distinguishes the track with angry honks and squawks, while the band maintains a truly industrial groove and flow to their stomp.

'Wait' (Reed)

After the acerbic double-barrel assault of the previous two tracks, things end on a lighter tone. Lou sings in his most fey, affected voice, while Marty Fogle guides the band through a post-doo wop exercise. The lyrics sung by Lou bump up against and clash with the words sung by the backing vocalists, competing for the listener's attention. A similar thing happens with the melody, bantered about by both sax and guitar, not quite playing the same figures. Little matter, as the song seems to focus on a lover, or pair of lovers who might want to 'wait' before someone changes their mind. On its own, it's dreck, but coming at the end of such a dark, intense album, it functions almost as a palate cleanser of sorts, with its 'girl group' bounce and airy sentiment. As the band wraps things up, the backing singers reference the Shirelles' 1958 hit 'Met Him on a Sunday', for reasons not wholly clear, but it works. Thus ends *Street Hassle*.

Live: Take No Prisoners (1978)

Personnel:
Lou Reed: vocals, guitar, Roland guitar synthesizer
Stuart Heinrich: guitar, backing vocals
Marty Fogle: electric saxophone
Michael Fonfara: Yamaha electric piano
Ellard 'Moose' Boles: bass, backing vocals
Michael Suchorsky: drums
Angela Howell: tambourine, backing vocals
Chrissy Faith: backing vocals
Recorded at: The Bottom Line, New York City, 17-21 May 1978
Producer: Lou Reed
Mixed and engineered at: Delta Studio, Wilster, DE, by Manfred Schunke
Audience engineer: Greg Caruso, Jay W. Krugman, and Julie Last
Assistant engineer: René Tinner
Release date: November 1978
Running time: 98:27
Highest chart places: US/UK: did not chart

The Bottom Line was a 400-seat music club on West 4th Street between Mercer and Greene in Greenwich Village that ran from 1974 to 2003. Its relatively intimate setting made it a favorite of both artist and fan for its nearly 30-year history. Lou certainly held the place in high regard and would play there whenever available. As the second of three LPs recorded with the Binaural Sound technology, this close, amenable atmosphere is certainly present on *Live: Take No Prisoners*, where Lou goads and guiles an appreciative, inebriated audience with full force. Long dismissed as a 90-plus-minute speed rap, the reality is that this is a vivid and glorifying live testament to Lou at his performative best – a *true Lou* statement, raw and unsanitized. This album is known and remembered, not so much for the songs played but rather, for what Lou *says* within each song. He is wired and on fire here, and his missives to the crowd drift freely and abruptly from the inane to the profound, often within the same sentence. As mentioned, this series of shows happened at the end of the tour, and the band is adept and well-seasoned to follow their leader through whatever twists and turns his scattershot whimsy dictates. Make no mistake, the band here is triple hot shit; this is the first, and unfortunately, last opportunity we get to hear The Everyman Band in full flight. Bassist Bruce Yaw has been replaced by Ellard 'Moose' Boles, a towering man well-versed in holding down the bottom end. Sax player Marty Fogle certainly gets his due with several opportunities to riff unfettered, and it is to our benefit. Lest there be any doubt, drummer Michael Suchorsky bends and shapes the groove to his will with strength and aplomb while always keeping it interesting.

And this LP is most certainly interesting, an album like no other. While it can share some similarities with other less-than-cordial live documents, such as The Stooges' *Metallic K.O.*, or The Misfits' *Evillive*, this one is unique, and it has its own legends. The album's title was apparently inspired by a fan in Quebec who was front-and-center for a show and kept cajoling Lou and the band to 'Take no prisoners!' before repeatedly slamming his head, face first, on the table at which he was sitting. A more controversial legend centers around the idea that in order to put this album together, Lou essentially gave all the raw performance tapes to Michael Fonfara and said 'Here'; the album that exists is the result of Fonfara's editing, sequencing, and remixing, not Lou's. This idea is something that Lou took some trouble to try and repress, seen especially when he wielded dictatorial editorial control over the liner notes of his retrospective box set some years later. Released in time for the Holiday Season, *Live: Take No Prisoners* avoided the charts, and despite doing so, it can coast on reputation alone, and it continues to. But as the wheels of commerce grind on, it was time to go back into the studio.

'Sweet Jane' (Reed)

The sound of fumbling for wooden matches, one being struck and igniting on the second pass, and the unmistakable sound of the quick exhale that follows a newly-lit cigarette, is the aural focus that greets us at this album's start. Lou then casually apologizes for some sort of tardiness: 'Hello… sorry we were late, but we were just tuning'. We are then dropped center stage at The Bottom Line. Amongst a lively and vocal scene, Lou promptly establishes terms with the audience. While commenting on how the stagehand who secured his vocal mic must be Godzilla, he indicates that in order to properly reach his mic, he must either 'grow an inch or… meet a boyfriend'. If the principles of Binaural Sound are to be believed, a drawling audience member on the right side of the stage repeatedly asks, 'A what… need a what?' After the briefest of pauses, Lou answers said inquiry with 'A boyfriend! Can't you fucking hear? What is wrong with you?', to rapturous applause. It is this initial exchange that sets the tone for the whole two-LP set. He then goes on to misquote, correct himself, and then properly quote William Butler Yeats' closing lines of the first stanza of *The Second Coming*, and then posits to the audience, 'Now you figure out where I am'. Once again, ecstatic applause ensues.

An audible count-in takes place, and the band snap-clicks into a vigorous and muscular version of this classic song. Lou takes broad liberties with the words and phrasing on this tune, as he does with most other tracks on the album. He bounces in and out of the lyrical narrative at will, and what is fueling and stoking this will is anybody's guess. The band is primed and fully fueled, ready to follow their boss anywhere, over any terrain. At 4:20, Lou shovels shit on Barbara Streisand for a comment she had made at that year's Academy Awards about how she wanted to thank 'all the little people' who made it all possible, etc., etc. After much riffing and kibbitzing, at 6:50, he asks himself, 'Are you political, Lou?' He follows this up with a question about what, specifically, there is to be political about, before delivering the t-shirt, bumper sticker, billboard-worthy declaration of 'Give me an issue, I'll give you a tissue… I'll wipe my ass with it'. Once more, at 7:20, Lou asks if this particular show is being broadcast. He then gets in a subtle dig at Patti Smith with 'Fuck Radio Ethiopia, man, I'm Radio Brooklyn… I ain't no snob, man!', and the room explodes. After putting drummer Michael Suchorsky through some on-the-spot, ad hoc changes, things conclude with great fanfare. All things considered, this is a truly great reading of a truly great song.

'I Wanna be Black' (Reed)
Before the ink had even dried on the previous track, Michael Fonfara is tapping out the two-step riff on electric piano. Michael Suchorsky kicks up sixteenths on the floor tom to bring the band to attention, and the whole ensemble leaps into full flourishment. Make no mistake, this is a rock band that can *swing*, and swing they do with strength and ease on this track, every voice bouncing and swaying with effortless poise. Stuart Heinrich is first to step forward with a very tasty and tasteful, urban and urbane, active solo that at first suffers from its subdued placement in the mix. Halfway through, he remembers his amp's gain knob, and he begins to cut glass. Not once does he overstep or misjudge; there is action, speed, and flash in his solo, yet restraint rides shotgun throughout. This goes on for several bars before the baton is passed to Marty Fogle. In his many years of employment with Lou, this is his first chance on record to truly step out, and step out he does. Measurable standards of sleaze and grease drip from the bell of his horn as he coats the audience with an RnB solo that boldly tattles to the teacher. Not one note is falsified, not one riff is rushed, and it is the easiest and most revolting pleasure for your ears. Angela Howell and Chrissy Faith join him on backing vocals, harmonizing the song's title rhythmically.

By the time Lou gets involved, the song is half over. After much clowning, Lou quizzes Mses. Howell and Faith on their impressions of various black men. First on the list is James Brown, who elicits a microphone-overdriving shriek. Next, curiously, is André Previn, who is most certainly not black. When asked who he is, Lou responds, 'He's French', to which Ms. Howell says, 'Oh… just as well'. High jinks, all around. At the close of the first and only chorus in the song, Lou clears the decks for the song's conclusion with a kidney stone-loosening bellow that allows the band to pause before bringing it home. Despite this song's potentially troublesome lyrics and ideas, this is a joyous and raucous rendition from a band at full tilt in front of a crowd that just cannot get enough, and it is rigorously infectious.

'Satellite of Love' (Reed)
This song's previous live outing on record missed the mark – here, it takes flight. While the first two tracks on side one are programmed to resemble a consistent performance, this song comes to us after a pause between the

previous track and this one. Michael Fonfara leads us in through his piano intro before the band comes crashing in with great fanfare. This is a full-blooded, rock 'n' roll reading of this song, to be sure, and its energy sustains throughout the performance, courtesy of the band. Lou refrains from too much banter with the crowd on this number; he tends to generally stick to the script here. With two minutes to go, Lou fires up his Roland guitar synthesizer for added raunch as the rest of the players do their part to bring the song to the finish line.

'Pale Blue Eyes' (Reed)
What was once a gentle folk ballad gets its long overdue RnB reading here. Starting off side two of the original LP sequence, Lou once again revs up his guitar synthesizer to make his guitar sound like… an accordion. His vocal performance has a raw integrity to it; he means it here, and the backing vocals of Mses. Howell and Faith add to this conviction. Again, he sticks to the script here without a great deal of audience engagement. At 4:30, Marty Fogle leans in with a closing-credits-of-*Saturday Night Live* sax solo that amply pushes things over the top, but in a good way. For those who might have found the original version on the third VU album a bit too sleepy, they will find the antidote here.

'Berlin' (Reed)
Another discontinuous recording, this performance adheres more closely to the *Lou Reed* version as opposed to its namesake representation from a few years later. While the listener is gratifyingly spared the 'one sweet day' rave-up at the close of the inaugural LP's version, and the atmospheric oddities of the *Berlin* album that are almost untranslatable to the stage in 1978, this still means there is the inclusion of the verse that mentions hiring a vet, although here it has been changed to marrying a vet. The key here is the band; they maintain a whisper-clear vibe during the verses and then elevate to a thunderous roar during the choruses. While Lou, once again, avoids the cantankerous crowd engagement that this album's reputation rests upon, he spits out his lines with fire and belief, while Marty Fogle again gets a fine lyrical solo in, and the backing singers add their distinct polish at every turn. This is perhaps the perfect marriage between the two very unique and very different versions of this song, meeting somewhere in the middle with both performance and atmosphere in this truly unique reading of this classic Lou song.

'I'm Waiting For the Man' (Reed)
The last three songs have been somewhat by-the-book, performance-wise, in terms of variation and/or audience engagement. Here, affairs are returned to the mood and aura that this live LP's reputation is based upon, gloriously so. Fading in mid-song from some other planetary realm, the band is deep in a

cool simmer as Lou hisses and rasps us through the familiar tale that passes along the factual and crucial information that The Man is never early, he's always late. Stuart Heinrich spits and snarls behind his singer with riffs that flare up in the murk like flash paper. Very early on, Lou begins to wander, and in come the quips and jibes. The groove simmers to just bass and drums, and the crowd starts to announce their enthusiasm. Lou meets this with 'I sing when you shut up'. We further hear about how he gives you a sweet taste, but he has to split because 'don' 'cho know, somebody else is waiting for the man', and the band and backing singers begin to rise in intensity. At this point, Lou starts to lyrically shift gears, as he tells some 'bitch' she 'better get out of here quick'. He continues with the slurred declaration of 'You read (sic) too many movies, baby, you read... too many of your college plays', and it becomes clear that we are on the bus to 'Temporary Thing' town. At 4:51, he finally makes the long-delayed announcement that 'it's just a Temporary Thing', to raucous crowd affirmation. Lou squeezes out some crucial crunch chords from his guitar and the band follows suit with another elevation in intensity, before finally falling into a chorus of sorts, and then just as quickly and deftly lowering back down to a murmur. Lou expounds:

> ...nobody's got you tied down to the fucking bed, man, if you don't like it around here just get the fuck away. I'm on top of the world today, honey... I don't need you, NOBODY, and don't you bring me down. It's just a temporary thing. I KNOW.

After further castigation of additional errors and issues, he once again comes to sing the song's title and is joined by the backing singers, while Marty Fogle steps in and pimps it up a bit. At 9:15, Lou states, 'I'm waiting for my man'. He goes into an interesting and clearly improvised account of the erratic and, at times, tempestuous relationship between dealer and user:

> He be here, either now or never... it's always never, man; even when he's here, it's never... very funny thing about that; even when I have it, I don't have it. I never figured that out... all fucking day after night, fucking asshole gets stuck in a taxi... and I'm fucking SITTING there... asshole... fucking call!

Lou returns to the 'Temporary Thing' narrative once again, and then randomly mentions Groucho Marx and his quote, 'Bring me a rose, or leave me alone', as a metaphor for the shit he does not want to take from his partner. The band then spends the next several bars rising to a loud and energized climax, which the audience repays with noisy appreciation. This is perhaps the most 'live' track on the album; it positively sweats and gasps with rock 'n' roll atmosphere. Condensation drips down the walls of this track; the listener can smell the smoky, musky club interior while they see and hear a band bleeding out the groove. It's a shame that this track is faded in, as the full performance must be truly rich to behold.

'Coney Island Baby' (Reed)

Side three of the set starts off with Michael Fonfara's electric piano picking out the two-chord melody and the band following Michael Suchorsky's tumbling toms into the groove. Marty Fogle flits about with whisps of riffs before Lou begins his recount of high school athletic aspirations. Lou mentions various towns and communities on Long Island and the members of the audience who have been repeatedly calling out, 'Lou! Freeport High' get their due. The hushed intimacy of the studio version is naturally missing here, but the band handles it with delicacy and grace. Lou takes some broad and casual liberties with his timing and phrasing of the words, suggesting a casual connection to the performance, if not blatant Vegas-style showmanship. Nevertheless, things erupt into seismic blasts at the chorus, with Lou absolutely roaring out about the princess on the hill, only to instantly and magically drop back into softness in order to properly be told about the glory of love.

At 5:08, with three-and-a-half minutes left in the song, the band begins a muscular and extended vamp, repeating 'The Glory of Love' while Lou howls like a possessed sage unburdening himself of his message. It is a vigorous performance.

'Street Hassle' (Reed)

How does such a rich studio creation come off onstage? Beginning with the spirited banter of Lou claiming that people will accuse him of having 'mellowed' because he is so verbose on stage, he then follows that with: 'He didn't act mean. He talked … we'll mug you later. Feel better?' He then repeatedly triggers a feedback noise on his guitar and/or microphone, asking the audience, 'Isn't that annoying?' He calls out to the two owners of The Bottom Line, Allan Pepper and Stanley Snadowsky, 'Monitor! Monitor, are you paying attention? Allan and Stanley, these are your microphones!' After a few more squeals, 'That's how *Metal Machine* was born, by the way'. A bit more banter later, where certain vocal audience members are advised to 'Go leave if you don't like it', an on-stage count-off leads to this song's memorable and crucial three-note signifier, brusquely and deftly played by Michael Fonfara and Moose Boles. The guitars fall in, along with crisp cymbal washes and saxophone calls.

Lou walks us through the tale of Waltzing Matilda and The Sexy Boy with a tactile sense of importance, renewing the vitality of the lovers' tale for the sake of the performance. Mses. Howell and Faith are crucial to the proceedings, as are the backing vocals on the studio version. At the close of the song's first part, things are neat and tidy. It is at this point that Angela Howell and Chrissy Faith step forward and offer their pure, unaccompanied, wordless testament to the narrative of *Street Hassle*. Their vocals float above the tight, hot confines of the rock 'n' roll club into the greater atmosphere, effortlessly and ethereally.

At their conclusion, Lou cannot be helped but mention 'That was beautiful', because it is. The audience agrees, and Moose Boles leads the riff on loud and proud bass. Marty Fogle joins him on the riff and Michael Suchorsky experiments with the rhythm on his cymbals. Lou leads us through the troublesome and difficult second section of the song by really playing up the drama of the characters involved in the scenario of how to dispose of a newly deceased corpse. He truly transcends any kind of performative aspect of the song to deliver a real conversational reality to his delivery, as if Lou was speaking to you directly about how it's your responsibility to get your dead girlfriend the fuck out of his apartment.

As on the studio version, things abruptly stop when Lou declares Bad Luck; Moose Boles has hit the overdrive setting on his amp, and his bass roars into part three. One by one, the instruments and voices rise and coalesce to a near cacophony that has barely enough room for Lou to declare that love has slipped away. Things rage on to a nearly *White Light/White Heat* level of intensity before they just as quickly and effortlessly break to the song's denouement. As shown, in the right hands, this piece comes off onstage just as crucially as its studio manifestation.

'Walk on the Wild Side' (Reed)

Here we get a history lesson, among other things. Starting side four with a chorus of standard on-stage tuning tones, Lou regales us with how a disgruntled patron – 'We had some nut here the other night, man' – tried to confront Lou after the show. 'I wanna talk to that fucking Lou Reed, man; why'd he throw a cup at his roadie?' Lou then explains that there is no place onstage to place his drink, so he rests it on the floor, out of the way. Apparently, this audience member saw it differently and raised such a fuss that five cops were called, and the guy went so far as to hit one of them. Big laughs. Lou hooks and jabs with the crowd a bit more before stating that his engagement has lasted for an entire week thus far.

> You think that's an accomplishment? I think it's, y'know ... something you're sentenced to. And if you don't get that, you get the Palladium ... two hours with 14,000 animals throwing beer cans at you.

At just over two minutes in, Michael Fonfara begins the two-chord vamp that makes clear what song is up next. Mass approval ensues. Once the groove is settled, Lou kibbitzes with his band, making idle threats: 'Don't you show any passion! You show an emotion, I fire you!' He states that he is unsure if he has actually done this song at all during the week's engagement and reaffirms his audience commitment by claiming that he has no problem playing 'your favorites', but as to be expected, 'there's just so many favorites to choose from'. This, too, gets a big laugh.

At 3:41 into the song, we finally hear the first line about Holly and her origins. This is all we get for a time, as Lou continues to wax mercurial, getting truly weird at some points; topics include sex with a brontosaurus, how 'nothing' is a 'style', what you might want to do on a Saturday night, and, most tellingly, 'Watch me turn into Lou Reed before your very eyes. AW! I do Lou Reed better than anybody, so I thought I'd get in on it'. Exactly one minute after its conceptual debut, Lou repeats his lyrical intro with Holly Woodlawn, this time finishing the verse and culminating with the chorus, all the while swerving and careening in and out of rhythm, tempo, and phrasing like a king in his castle.

Next, he asks the crowd if they would like to know how the song got written, and he takes us through his halls of memory, touching on the 'first time I quit rock 'n' roll because of too many lawsuits', referencing Summer 1970, his stint as a typist at his father's accounting firm, and the ups and eventual downs of writing for a doomed stage production. As per usual, quips and zingers abound, pausing only to say hello to Bruce Springsteen, who was an attendant for that night's performance. Like the inebriated potentate that he was, Lou bestows his blessing on Mssr. Springsteen, with

Springsteen is alright, by the way. He gets my seal of approval. I think he's groovy. You notice the way the critics turned him right after they were on him, right? When he needed them, they weren't there at any time.

This statement can be seen as the warm-up pitch for one of *Take No Prisoners'* greatest themes: Lou's outright assault on music critics.

Critics. What does Robert Christgau do in bed? What is he, a toe fucker? ... Man, A Consumer's Guide to Rock, what a moron! I object to the fucking liner notes! ... John Rockwell, man. Wow! You know how heavy it is to be reviewed by Rockwell? He says you're intelligent. Fuck you! I don't need you to tell me that I'm good! ... He writes and studies at Harvard... OPERA! A fucking opera guy, man! And that's the critic for *The New York Times* that makes and breaks the best rock bands that are very heavy and intelligent ... Christgau's like an anal retentive. Nice little boxes. B+. Can you imagine working for a fucking year and you got a B+ from an asshole in The Village Voice? You don't have to take this shit; you don't have to talk to the fucking journalists. They get in for free.

This rumbles on for a while as Lou is fully gassed and primed for trouble, most certainly laying out concrete evidence of his reputation as punk rock's errant father with attitude to spare. All the while, the band patiently, meticulously holds the groove, with Michael Suchorsky slapping it out on the closed high hat, Marty Fogle honoring the melody on his horn, and Michael Fonfara laying out chords on the keys.

At 7:46, the second set of verses finally comes into focus while Lou briefly recalls Candy Darling: 'I really miss Candy, and I didn't even know her that well; I'm such a scam artist'. He wastes little time before he gets to Little Joe, whom we are informed is 'an idiot, I don't know if any of you know that'. This character riff naturally comes around to mentioning Warhol, and here Lou drops the guises, if only momentarily. 'Andy has taken himself away from us, and he's right! Now I know why he did it! So, Drella, if you're there … I'm very glad that you're around', he calmly states, and he sounds like he means it. Gore Vidal, Norman Mailer, Sugarplum Fairy, and others all get a namecheck, delving deeply into the cozy alliances of the NYC literary glitterati as the band plays on. By the time he gets around to Jackie Curtis, the wind is beginning to sag from the sails; at 16:55, this song is the two-LP set's longest number, and it begins to show.

At 12:16, Lou references 'the colored girls', thus bringing us to the 'doot-de-doos', only to briskly cut them off to remind the audience, and himself, of his mission to once again attempt to explain the song's origin. The story and its details ramble forward in a sideways fashion before Lou, sated with his recitation, lets the band fade into a whisper, curiously followed by a total lack of end-of-song applause. This live version is certainly an improvement over the previous version on *Lou Reed Live*, but it plays almost like a comedy record in that it's great the first time when the 'jokes' are new, yet ages rapidly with each successive listen. The same criticism could justifiably be leveled at the entire album, but this track shows the strain the quickest.

'Leave Me Alone' (Reed)

Oddly wrapping up with this in-concert onslaught, the granite-crumbling stomp of Lou's guitar rawness sets the stage. Coming at nearly twice the original studio version's tempo, there is vicious *sturm und drang* aplenty from all participants. Lou sputters out the words in a barely intelligible spurt from verse to verse. Stuart Heinrich gets in an especially ripping solo through the fog of battle; his presence has been fairly low-key on this album, and here he gets to really blaze, while the background vocalists keep things tethered to the floor with their 'Huh! Oh, yeah!' contributions. At 3:40, Michael Fonfara gets a dynamic and long-delayed electric piano solo that is tragically buried in the mix. This is truly unfortunate; as band leader and rhythmic anchor for the band, his work is consistently exemplary, but rarely does he get a chance to really wail, and he does so here with riffs and phrases that run the gamut of tension and release, if we could only hear more of them. The song's enhanced tempo is merely catnip to his abilities. The flame is reduced at 5:10 as we begin to prepare for landing, with just over two minutes left. The players begin to get a bit abstract in their notes and chords – perhaps fatigue is setting in? At 6:10, one final string of verses is launched before things crash to the ground in a typical end-of-performance cacophony. Curiously, for an album that is so verbose, there is no 'Thank you, goodnight' statement of any kind here. It's just over.

The Bells (1979)

Personnel:

Lou Reed: lead and backing vocals, electric guitar, guitar synthesizer, bass synthesizer (track 8), horn arrangement

Ellard 'Moose' Boles: 12-string electric guitar (track 8), bass guitar, bass synthesizer, backing vocals

Michael Fonfara: piano, Fender Rhodes, synthesizer, backing vocals, executive producer

Don Cherry: African hunting guitar, trumpet, horn arrangement (track 4)

Marty Fogle: ocarina, soprano and tenor saxophone, Fender Rhodes (track 9), horn arrangement

Michael Suchorsky: percussion

Produced at: Delta Studios, Wilster, West Germany, by Lou Reed

Engineer: René Tinner

Mixing: Manfred Schunke

Mastering: Ted Jensen

Release date: April 1979

Running time: 40:37

Highest chart places: US: 130, UK: did not chart

This is a weird one; neither 'good weird' nor 'bad weird', just *weird*. It is the third and, some might say, thankfully final LP recorded in the Binaural Sound method, as Manfred Schunke's presence here will signify. The album was completely recorded in his studio on the rural outskirts of West Germany. Of the three LPs recorded with this method, this one has the strangest sound, particularly Lou's vocals, which have a puzzling, aluminum foil essence to them, causing the mix to almost sound unfinished or incomplete. A similar aural effect can be heard on Leonard Cohen's 'glorious failure', *Death of a Ladies Man*, where Phil Spector barred Cohen from the studio after laying down mere scratch vocal tracks. While the tracks on *The Bells* themselves are fine, if not serviceable, a sense of incompletion lurks in the periphery on account of the curious placement and tone of the vocals. Lou's actual singing also calls for assessment here; he employs a generally heretofore unused vocal vibrato that greatly boosts the dramatic essence of each performance. Strictly speaking, there is drama to spare here. Lou revs himself up to such a lather on some songs that he sounds almost comical at times as if he was a character on some insufferable sitcom or cartoon show. Really, this is not an exaggeration.

As for the actual songs, they take on a confessional quality that suggests a certain tenderness or sense of mercy, whether it is mercy desired, or mercy bestowed. Writing began around Thanksgiving of 1978, and it yielded curious results, as members of the band received broad, sweeping co-writing credit – a first for Lou since the days of the VU. Lou only claims one song as wholly his own. Guitarist Nils Lofgren had been cowriting with Lou, and three of their pieces would appear here, with the remainder showing up on Lofgren's fifth LP. While Lofgren does not play on the album, an even more significant presence here is that of jazz innovator Don Cherry. While a student at Syracuse, Lou often played Cherry's music on his radio show. Now, many years later, to have Cherry play onstage and in the studio with him was a true triumph.

As stated, *The Bells* is a weird one; it has divided listeners and critics over the years, with its weak points usually outweighing its strong points. Due to the lack of anything even resembling a single, Arista put almost no promotion behind it, and it disappeared after a brief low-chart presence. Naturally, Lou blamed yet another commercial failure on all within his field of vision, claiming that his best album of all time had been neglected. He toured the album with his band and made the best of it, but changes were in store, beyond just the music.

The Bells can be called, unironically, Lou's last speed album, as he was to begin a long, slow journey toward sobriety that would last for the next few years after the album's conclusion. While his speed usage would wax and wane over the years of his usage, Victor Bockris, in his *Transformer: The Lou Reed Story*, details what Lou's peak usage was in the 1970s:

> Standard practice for the group was to shoot up first thing in the morning and then at some other point later in the day. The shots were so strong as to be considered lethal by conventional medical standards. A forged prescription of Desoxyn, for example, would consist of a bottle of a hundred yellow pills, of the highest (15 mg) potency. The ordinary recommended dosage, adjusted, of course, to meet the needs of the individual, was fifteen to twenty-five milligrams orally per day. The Lister (Bob Lister, the person at the center of this group of users) amphetamine circle, on the other hand, would habitually use ten to twenty 15 mg pills at once and inject them directly into the bloodstream. These men were not messing about.

Strong stuff, to be sure. Lou did not necessarily want to give up speed, but it was simply becoming harder to get, so why not make a break for it. After all, there was still plenty of booze in no short supply. Very soon, Lou's speedy, stick-like frame became saddled with a boozer's bloat. The drinking would eventually be shown the door as well, due to a doctor's firm suggestion, but not just yet – there were other changes afoot. Rachel was in the hind view, and Lou had met Sylvia Morales: the radiant, cultured, intelligent and well-traveled fashion designer of the NYC nightlife scene. She would eventually become Lou's second wife, with all that such a union entails: manager, nursemaid, confidant, babysitter, punching bag, etc. Between the release of *The Bells* and Lou's next LP, 1980s *Growing Up in Public*, they would wed and buy a secluded home in the rural removes of Blairstown, New Jersey. At that point, Lou would fully embrace sobriety and begin a series of albums that would offer a new, thoroughly pronounced and deeply profound string of work for the 1980s. But we are not there yet.

'Stupid Man' (Reed, Nils Lofgren)

Prancing piano chords drop us into what can only be seen as some kind of Long Island soap opera scenario, with quavering, heartfelt vocals to boot. Lou passionately sings of an errant father, the song's 'Stupid Man', making a distanced greeting to the daughter that he promises he will soon be a proper parent to. The band provides a solid bed for him to sing on, and little else. That dynamic is very prevalent on this album; not unlike a hip-hop MC styling over a DJ track, the band here lays down a foundation and stays out of the way, by and large. Marty Fogle and Don Cherry's horn charts add propulsion, but the album's overall sound, as first evidenced here, is really a puzzler. The drums, particularly the snare, sound gated to the point of Styrofoam, the piano sounds sub-aquatic, and the vocals sound unfinished. Things do improve as we move on.

'Disco Mystic' (Reed, Boles, Fogle, Fonfara, Suchorsky)

Disco, Disco Mystic. That's it, really. Judging from all players receiving a co-writing credit, this must have emerged out of an in-studio jam. In allegiance to the title, there are swirling synthesized strings, emphasis on the hi-hat, and effect-treated guitars. Lou repeats the song's title in a low-register bullfrog croak, and not for the last time on the album, either. Between choral recitation of the song's title, Marty Fogle bleats out a sax line, fed through some type of modulation, that is just so squalid and sleazy that it almost makes the rest of the exercise justifiable. Almost. At 4:29, it is overlong. Disco, Disco Mystic.

'I Want to Boogie With You' (Reed, Fonfara)

A boxed-in attempt at Spector-esque RnB. The band holds a conjured, synthesized aluminum Wall of Sound groove while the vocals sound as if they have been collected from the finishing tray of a Xerox machine. The lyrics detail someone's pleas to get someone else to give them a try, romantically, despite strong discouragement from other parties. At 2:51, Lou gets in a solo that carries on to the song's conclusion; it is unmistakable Lou-on-guitar, tone-wise, note-wise, and feel-wise.

'With You' (Reed, Lofgren)

With this song, the drama ascends to high dudgeon. Lou's experimentation with vocal styling on this album reaches its apex here; at certain parts, he is amped up to a level of near hysteria, resembling, perhaps, a festive older family member in a Woody Allen film, or, perhaps, a troubled neighbor on a Seinfeld episode, *kvetching* about their ungrateful niece and their *shpilkes*, how this only adds to their unrelenting *tsuris*, and *oy* this heat. Lou squawks and bleats through lines that rhyme 'capricious' with 'death wish', and, yes, just like Annette Funicello, 'illusion' with 'contusions'. However, all is not lost here; this tale of squabbling lovers has its share of points: 'With you, everyone's a sucker/With you, it's fuckee or fucker/Slow down, slow down'. A burbling synth bass keeps things active, and there does seem to be a disproportionate number of chord changes in this song; this, along with the horns, is perhaps where *The Bells* gets its reputation as Lou's 'jazziest' LP.

'Looking For Love' (Reed)
Lou's only solo creation here is the album's only real rocker – and a real rocker it is. Starting with a guitar and sax duet, the band comes thundering in, and Lou roars out his words as if he were back onstage at The Bottom Line, all chemically fueled up and ready. His performance is of such a raw and uncaged variety that most of the words from this tale of compromised lovers seeking compromised lovers are lost. No matter – that's rock 'n' roll, and he is feeling it. There is a curious lyrical twist buried within the lovely girl/lonely boy antics:

I said hey now, you used to scratch my back
And you look across the board
Hey now, when you ripped open my shirt
You see that's written hey 'The Wanderer' on my chest

This specificity is incongruous with the rest of the song's standard he/she ideas. Marty Fogle gets a pair of fully sanctified Steve Douglas-style solos that up the rock 'n' roll quotient exponentially. This song could have been a single from an otherwise single-less album if not for the icy, fractious mix that is dominant throughout the LP. At the same time, Billy Joel was doing much more with far less.

'City Lights' (Reed, Lofgren)
To finish side one of the LP, Lou returns to his dime-store, Lou Rawls bullfrog croak to praise Charlie Chaplin. A light piano-driven tune lays the foundation for Lou to frequently refer to the very film that is widely considered to be Chaplin's finest in the song's title. The song is an overall celebration of The Little Tramp and his impish appeal, yet in the middle verse, there is a curious element:

Charlie Chaplin's little cane, well it flicked away the rain
Things weren't quite the same, after he came here
But then when he left, upon our own request
Things weren't quite the same, after he came here
We're supposed to be
A land of liberty

In his biography, Anthony De Curtis astutely points to these lines as a lamentation over Chaplin's continued harassment by the CIA and its horrid, self-hating leader, J. Edgar Hoover. This ultimately resulted in Chaplin's banishment from the United States, despite being a creative figure of great cultural magnitude who brought wise joy to generation upon generation of viewers. Without beating the listener over the head with raw tales of injustice, the ideas are offered in a song that is as light on its feet as The Little Tramp was.

'All Through the Night' (Reed, Don Cherry)

The beginning of the LP's second side starts with the same kind of mid-party atmosphere that appeared on 'Dirt' from *Coney Island Baby* four years previous. Various voices and doings rise and fall in the audible spectrum while the band lays into an easy, non-threatening vibe, and the horn bleats out a simple repetitive riff that suggests a theme from an educational children's program. When Lou comes in, it sounds as if his vocal mic is down the hall and to the left, but he doesn't lack feeling. He sings of tales of the luckless and troubled, rounding off each circumstance with the placement of 'all through the night'. Some are lyrical, some banal, some infantile, but Lou sings them all with truth.

> When the words were down and the poetry comes and
> the novel's written and the book is done you said oh lord,
> lover baby give it to me all through the night and she says it

This is a curious meditation, as is:

> If the sinners sin and the good man's gone and a woman can't come
> And help him home and what you gonna do about it
> When they go on all through the night

Lou has visited these kinds of figures many times, but usually with stronger results, such as on *Street Hassle*. The characters here get a kind of all-purpose glossing over; there is a lack of directness in the recounting of their struggles, despite evidence of its presence:

> I went to St. Vincent's and I'm watching the ceiling
> fall down on the body as she's lying there on the ground
> Says oh baby, gotta celebrate all through the night

This certainly lends credence to the concern, but that's as far as it goes. Despite his impassioned and wavering vocals, the connection to the narrative comes off as noncommittal. Don Cherry gets a co-writing credit here, but his contribution is vague, as this song is another one of the album's examples of Lou singing over a looped phrase with no musical change throughout.

'Families' (Reed, Boles)

The family, one of Lou's most frequently visited sources of consternation, is given the full treatment here. However, the rage that typifies such songs is absent, replaced by a timid and hopeful request for acceptance. Like the previous song, it consists of one musical idea repeated infinitely while Lou does his thing over the top. Background vocals recurrently ask, 'How's the family?', at the close of each verse, while Lou bleats and warbles in a voice drenched and suffocating in performative emotion. This can be a bit hard to take, especially when Lou starts simpering 'Mama!' and 'Papa!' at the song's close, but his words say a great deal about the many kinds of acknowledged and obscured difficulties that can occur in any family; the secrets and lies that even the most loving of groups can share, both consciously and unconsciously:

> And Mama, I know how disappointed you are
> And Papa, I know that you feel the same way, too
> And no, I still haven't got married
> And no, there's no grandson
> Planned for you
> And by the way daddy, tell me how's the business
> I understand that your stock she's growing very high
> No daddy, you're not a poor man anymore
> And I hope you realize that
> Before you die

It's not necessary to know whether these words and ideas were actually exchanged by Lou and his parents. While many of the more direct grievances Lou has levelled at his parents over the years have been questioned – if not contradicted and negated – by intimates, the sheer weight of the feelings expressed reveal the song's true worth, all the while sung by a man who sounds close to the verge of tears.

> But Papa, I know that this visit's a mistake
> There's nothing here we have in common except our name
> And families that live out in the suburbs
> Often make each other cry
> And I don't think that I'll come home much anymore
> No, no I don't think I'll come home much again

The near-six-minute length of this song, along with its unchanging music, emotional vocal delivery, and sad subject matter, make it a formidable listen.

'The Bells' (Reed, Fogle)

This looming, syrupy, thick morass of experimentation is the last song on Lou's last album of the 1970s. At nearly nine-and-a-half minutes, there is plenty of room here. Both Marty Fogle and Don Cherry blow ample breath through their horns to rise and fall with the three-note bass dirge and hovering, misty keyboards. An untethered voice intones unintelligible words in the sonic gloom, similar to the bed of voices that glide throughout 'Murder Mystery' from the third VU album. The rich minor chords and spiraling horns are almost gothic in their sense of foreboding. At 5:30, Lou comes in with vocals, buried in the mix, that he claims were improvised on the spot, after hearing Marty Fogle rehearsing what became his keyboard line. As Lou sings, Michael Suchorsky pounds on the toms while a whistle-like synthesizer melody floats up. What does Lou sing of? He himself had gone on record as having no real idea as to what the words were about. Again, DeCurtis posits a 'meditation on the emotional fragility of performance... the vulnerability and dangers of the artistic life'. This makes sense when we consider such lines as:

> After the plays have gone down
> And the crowds have scattered around
> Through the city lights and the streets
> No ticket could be beat
> For the beautiful show of shows
> Ah, Broadway only knows... After soaring through the air
> With nothing to hold him there
> It was really not so cute
> To play without a parachute

After a maniacal chorus calling out, 'Here comes the bells!', the song concludes with thunderous toms and the crash of a gong; a close that is almost identical to the ending of his 1970s debut.

Growing Up in Public (1980)

Personnel:
Lou Reed: vocals, guitar
Michael Fonfara: keyboards, guitar
Chuck Hammer: guitar, guitar synthesizer
Michael Suchorsky: drums
Ellard 'Moose' Boles: bass guitar, backing vocals
Stuart Heinrich: guitar, backing vocals
Produced at: AIR Studios, Montserrat, by Lou Reed and Michael Fonfara
Engineer: Corky Stasiak
Assistant Engineer: Tony George
Release Date: April 1980
Running time: 36:39
Highest chart places: US: 158, UK: did not chart

This album is the sound of transition, as there are numerous transitions at play with regard to the music, how it is made, and how it is provided. There are several distinct firsts, lasts, and onlys related to this album. Recorded in January of 1980, Lou and company collectively decamped to George Martin's swank, state-of-the-art AIR studios on the Caribbean island of Montserrat. As previously mentioned, speed was out of the picture, but this only led to an increased booze intake, and the resort-like atmosphere of beach, bar, and bungalow tidings on hand at AIR only encouraged such indulgence. Michael Fonfara, who received co-writing credit on all eleven of the album's cuts, has freely admitted that both Lou and he were fully gassed as they worked on the songs during the day and recorded them at night, and as we will see, even the very titles of some of the songs speak to this. While George Martin himself was not involved with the recording, he was on hand as the studio's owner and manager, and he and his wife would dine with Lou and Sylvia every evening, giving his impressions on the work at hand, much to Lou's adoration. Gone are the murky, metallic, midrange-favoring dynamics of binaural sound; what exists here bears all the markings of how popular music would come to sound in the approaching decade, with bright highs and non-threatening lows, and a much wider palette of sound for each instrument to shine in. The band is given much more room to move around in, and they adjust formidably. This is the last album to feature anyone from The Everyman Band, some of whom had been with him for most of the decade. Lou would not work with any of these players again.

As for vocals, Lou still employs the showbiz vibrato of his last few albums, but it is tempered here with a greater range of emotions. At times, he snarls, growls, croons, clowns, and almost laughs; this is due to a generally stronger and more robust assortment of ideas and expressions that begin to appear in the lyrics of this album. His lyrics begin to expand to the breadth and complexity which he became known and respected for later in life. The theme of the family is thoroughly explored, embroidered upon, and even fictionalized here, as are the personally timely themes of romantic risk, romantic rejection, romantic strife, and, finally, romantic devotion. There is anger, fear, frustration, and worry here aplenty, yet this is also refreshingly measured against ideas of lightness, love, hope, completeness, and even goofy-assed silliness as well. Things are in transition.

Between the recording and the release of this album, Lou and Sylvia were wed and would remain so for well into the next decade. This would close a chapter on a large part of Lou's public life. Additionally, after this album was in the can, Lou was informed in no uncertain terms that his liver was damaged and that he needed to quit drinking completely. While he was not at all pleased to hear that he would have to give up the bottle, he entered rehab and quit the drink. After yet another tour to support *Growing Up in Public*, he played his final show with The Everyman Band at the Aquarian Theatre in L.A. on 22 November 1980. He would not enter a recording studio for another year.

Arista, once again, put next to no promotion behind the album, as to their ears, once again, there was no potential hit. No matter, as this would be Lou's last album for the label. His next LP, appearing in February 1982, would be on a new label, with a new band, a new sound, and would very much seem to feature the creations of himself: a new man. *Growing Up in Public*, with its many transitions, is not only an acknowledgment and letting go of the past but also a vivid and enthusiastic salute to that which seems forthcoming. Sylvia and sobriety clearly play no small role here. Lou Reed would begin the new decade with new attitudes, concerns, and issues, and he would face it all in his own frantic, intelligent, messy, and unique way. The music he created, as a result, bears this fruit.

How Do You Speak to an Angel' (Reed, Fonfara)
A light 'n' lively, sunny day piano intro greets us with soft bass and hi-hat taps before we are squarely told of:

A son who is cursed with a harridan mother
Or a weak simpering father at best
Is raised to play out the timeless classical motives
Of filial love and incest.

Well, shit – we're deep in it already. The chorus asks the age-old question of how such a maladjusted mutation as the song's narrator, possibly Lou, screws up the courage to talk to the highest object of his frenzied affections, possibly Sylvia. 'How do you speak to her/How do you dance on the head of a pin/When you're on the outside looking in', puts this universal lover's conundrum in vivid prose, thoroughly bolstered by the singer's exacting and articulate self-descriptions: 'How do you deal with your vague self-comprehension/

What do you do when you lie?' This, coupled with the jarring and alarming descriptions of the narrator's family background throw this internal struggle into high relief. Musically, the song goes through many changes, courtesy of Michael Fonfara, who is generally credited with the music and arrangement of the album, while Lou did the words and basic chords for each song. There are changes in tempo, structure, and arrangement that end up more closely resembling musical theatre than rock 'n' roll. This is an idea we will see often throughout the songs on this album.

'My Old Man' (Reed, Fonfara)
From a 'weak simpering father' in the previous song, we move on to a patriarchal tyrant who beats his wife while his son hides in fear. Lou nostalgically brings us through his boyhood, recounting being lined up alphabetically, 'Reagan, Reed, and Russo', in his Brooklyn schoolyard. He tells us that, as a child, he wanted to be just like his father, yet as he grew and saw the man in more evolved ways, he grew to hate him.

A son watches his father, being cruel to his mother
And makes a vow to return only when
He is so much richer, in every way so much bigger
That the old man will never hit anyone again

This sums up the thrust of the song succinctly. The actuality of these events in the Reed home have been amply refuted, least of all by Lou himself. Sid Reed was by all accounts a warm and kind man who never beat his wife, Toby – we, the listeners, are being subjected to artistic license here. The band kicks up an active MOR rock groove that is only enhanced by the brightness of the production; the fact that the mix has finally discovered Ellard 'Moose' Boles is a sonic revelation. As with the previous track, and, in fact, all tracks on this album, Lou leans into his performance. In the last minute of the song, as the backing vocals sing 'Just like my old man', Lou breaks out with a shouted addition of, 'And can you believe what he said to me/He said, Lou, why don't you act like a man?' while a synthesizer punches up a very era-appropriate counterweight.

'Keep Away' (Reed, Fonfara)
Revving up with a toothsome, gutbucket riff that would make Keef Riffhard blush, this frenetic rocker drops us mid-argument and brilliantly runs through the lists of manically compiled things and ideas that race through a lover's head when in the midst of a vicious quarrel with their partner: 'You keep your jealousy and your snide remarks to yourself/You know that I'm not seeing anybody else'. Lou's performance stays in the pocket, but just barely; he could burst out anytime and truly get away, just like he says he should. This could be the end of a relationship, or it could be the crucial 'first big

fight' of a new relationship. It matters not because here are precisely the kinds of frenzied, angry promises and random property divisions that pop up and explode at times like these between lovers:

Here's a yardstick you can measure me by
Here's a coupon, maybe there's something you want to buy
Here's a Band-Aid in case you cut your feet
Here's a rubber mallet you can use on your front teeth
Here's a gun no one uses anymore
And a bracelet made of some inexpensive ore
And if I don't keep my word you won't see me anymore

It sounds as if a junk drawer is hastily being cleaned out and emptied; the question, as corny as it may seem, is whether this is a physical junk drawer or an emotional one. An easy trap that anyone in a relationship can fall into in moments of strife is to abruptly 'call the whole thing off'. This can be seen as a hostile strike toward the other person, and it can also be a short-term means of protecting oneself from further emotional pain. Lou has further ideas:

I swear I'll keep away from dignity and pride
I'll keep away from abstracts I'll keep it all inside
Well, I'll just wrap me up in butter and melt me on a shelf
I'll fry in my own juices I'll become somebody else... Well, I'll just swear to keep away from everything that's good
I'll lie down in the gutter where I really should
I swear I'll light a candle to every modern foe
I swear I'll close the book on this and not see you anymore
'cause I just gotta get away

This is a great song. The words are clever, spirited, and vast, and the band sounds perfectly engaged without a sliver of overstepping. Michael Fonfara should have been allowed to wear the composer/producer's cap more frequently.

'Growing Up in Public' (Reed, Fonfara)
As stated, this is an album in transition, about transition. Lou was looking back, perhaps finally, in order to look fully forward, as he now, finally, felt he had something to look forward to. This song is an effective measure-taking of nearly a decade of fulfilling the song title's promise. An easy, loping reggae-lite rhythm, the kind that would become abundantly prevalent throughout the coming decade, adds a breezy movement, bolstered by nimble octave figures on bass. The foibles and pursuits of the various are addressed and cataloged uniformly, all falling under the idea of 'Growing up in public with your pants

down'. Throughout this album, there is clear and recurring evidence that Lou has really upped his word game – this song is no exception:

> Some people think being a man is unmanly
> And then some people think the whole concept's a joke
> But then some people think being a man is the whole point
> And some people wish that they'd never awoke
> Up from a dream of nightmarish proportions
> Down to a size neither regal or calm
> A Prince Hamlet caught in the middle between reason and instinct
> Caught in the middle with your pants down again

The games we play with masks, guises, routines, costumes, even our personalities, coming from a man who claimed in his youth not to have a personality; these are all so much grander and harder to live through while living a life of fame in public. Lou first tasted notoriety at 24; he was now quickly circling 40, and he had the rings and scars to show for it. This new complexity and vitality in his prose show this change as part of his evolution as an artist and as a person. Looking back has always been a cagey proposition for Lou; many an interview has quickly gone south due to a writer asking Lou to expand on some quote/deed/adventure from the past, only to have Lou shut the whole thing down in a flash. This song deftly addresses a wide swath of existence with a very fine brush.

'Standing on Ceremony' (Reed, Fonfara)
We are back amongst the family, *somebody's* family, and the heat is on. Amidst crashing minor chords, a family member is coldly castigated for their lack of manners and respect while the family matriarch slowly expires in the other room. Good times! Lou spits the words out with bitter remorse, savoring each hard consonant and syllable. The chorus is a repetition of 'We were always standing on ceremony'. The third verse functions as a bridge of sorts; the chords change, as does the scenery. From astride a barstool, the singer requests 'another pretty sad song for me' from the jukebox, while asking the barkeep to tell any potential callers that he hasn't been seen for weeks. He wraps up this request with, 'And this one here's on me'. For the final minute of the song, minor chords descend while a chorus calls out the song's title, and Michael Fonfara goes bananas on synth and electric piano.

'So Alone' (Reed, Fonfara)
Side two of the LP starts with this delightful, spirited piece of musical theatre. This song, along with the next, could easily fit in some godawful rom-com meet-cute scenario, if not for the pure, albeit hidden, Lou-ness of it all. This song is really a lot of fun. The lyrics are both accurate and hilarious, the band

is put through their paces tenfold, and at the end, the experience described
has a universal quality to it. The song's title, 'So Alone', is used to describe
the state we often find ourselves in when we are searching for love and we
think we just might have found it, but we're not sure yet. The back and forth,
the backwards and forwards, the give and take, the getting to know and
accept – all are struggles to face and hills to climb. After a certain degree of
experience and maturity, one tends to realize that 'falling in love' is no easy
surrender to mere emotional gravity. The more times you've been around the
racetrack, the harder those turns feel and the sharper those stops are. Despite
our devoted efforts toward connection, at first, they often result in less than
stellar success or possibly even backfire entirely. Not only do the lyrics of the
song address this brilliantly, but Lou outdoes himself in performance. You can
really see him on stage, prancing about in costume as the band vamps up the
changes behind him. A sample:

She calls on the phone
She says she doesn't want to be alone
She says it's making her neurotic
But please don't mistake it for being erotic
So all alone…
Can't you understand that it's frightening
When you hear women talking about castrating and hating men
Who wants to know about how you hate men … Sure, all men are beasts
Hey look, I'll sit here quietly and I'll stare at my feet
I don't blame you for taking umbrage
With animals staring at your cleavage
So alone

The song is sung in a bouncy, jovial, sing-song quality that often verges into
speech, giving the ideas a true sense of real performance. The band follows
adeptly; a sleazy disco groove is established as Lou demands his partner to
get up and dance in between near prog rock assaults of notes and drums.
The song concludes with both of the hopefully soon-to-be lovers exhausted
by their emotional badminton match, and the singer suggests sleep. Lou's
audible yawns put us over the edge of the story. Up to this point in his
recorded career, who knew he had such a flair for humor and the theatre?

'Love is Here to Stay' (Reed, Fonfara)
The cuteness valve has been kicked wide open for this gentle reminder of
how opposites attract. Triumphant guitar cadences announce the proceedings,
while the drums thunder and bark in anthemic celebration. Yet another 1980s
trope: stadium rock bombast, seen here in its infancy. Lou comes in singing
the song's title and then begins comparing and contrasting. Culinary habits,
reading habits, and spirituality-lite habits are mentioned, yet despite disparate

and overlapping tendencies, the two are in love, and it is here to stay. It is hard not to see this as a clear and obvious reflection of Lou and Sylvia's budding romance.

'The Power of Positive Drinking' (Reed, Fonfara)
A loose-limbed mid-tempo shuffle offers up this tongue-in-cheek meditation on alcoholism. These days were numbered for Lou, but he didn't know that yet. A kind of laughing-to-keep-from-crying humor flows throughout this song, aided and abetted by the irritating nursery rhyme chorus of 'The pow pow pow pow power of positive drinking'. The wisdom of the 'lovable lush' is on full display in the lyrics:

> Some people say alcohol makes you less lucid
> And I think that's true if you're kind of stupid
> I'm not the kind that gets himself burned twice
> And some say that liquor kills the cells in your head
> And for that matter so does getting out of bed
> When I exit, I'll go out gracefully, shot in my hand

This is the kind of easy braggadocio that is often used to justify self-abusive behaviors, and it was certainly indicative of the tenor of the times during its composition. The pleasant melody and easy sing-ability of the track further the mood of how it's really no big deal, so have another, why don't you? Don't mind if I do.

'Smiles' (Reed, Fonfara)
Yet another bright, bouncy groove welcomes us into a matter-of-fact study of the concealment of emotions. 'When I was young, my mother said to me'/'Never, ever let them see that you're happy'/Smiles, never, ever let them see you smile', is the idea here. It is suggested that there is weakness and vulnerability in a happiness exposed, and it is for the safety of the bearer to keep these things under wraps. Perhaps smiles can be seen as the apex of phoniness, the clear and glaring presence of contrived emotional artifice:

> Smiles-they all smile on TV
> The quizmaster with his withered crones
> The talk show hosting movie stars
> The politician licking feet
> The mugger, the rapist
> The arsonist lover
> All smile out form the news
> At one time or another
> Those smiles-those garish sickly smiles.

This would be a bit more believable if the words were not wedded to such a cheery, sunny, upbeat track. At 1:16, the players pause, and the piano begins a series of striding chords to build up a crescendo of sorts. Thundering, double-bass drum fills match the keys' activity, and this build-up lasts for 30 seconds. After many showy crashes and spurts, Lou comes back in and repeats his statement about the trouble of smiling, before ending with 'Don't you know they'll make you go: Doo doo doo doo doo, doo doo doo doo', parodying 'Walk on the Wild Side'. What the connection is between the two songs is anybody's guess.

'Think it Over' (Reed, Fonfara)

Despite his carefully and meticulously curated tough-guy-of-the-streets image, Lou was never one to scrimp on the romantic syrup. And while at first, this can seem cloying and icky, there is always a certain extra element present in his work, regardless of how obscured it may be. What seems like a simple, by-the-numbers 'Let's get married' song, actually has an emotional and intellectual depth that is typically absent from some of the more fairytale versions of such a situation, and this is first made clear in the song's title. While a marriage proposal is usually followed with immediate and exalted agreement when presented in a fable, here the asker proposes to the person being asked to merely 'think it over'. Rather than two late adolescents blissfully agreeing to what they both think will be a life with no more stress or worry or disagreement forever, here we have two adults who know better, yet still want all of each other. They know of the monumental importance of what they are considering; this cannot be decided impulsively or by emotion alone, so they must think it over:

> And the words that she first heard him speak
> Were really very sweet
> He was asking her to marry him, and to think it over
> Baby think it over.

She responds:

> Because when you ask for someone's heart
> You must know that you're smart
> Smart enough to care for it
> So I'm gonna think it over
> Baby, I'm going to think it over.

These words are served by the softest track on the album, with picked guitar, piano, deeply reverbed drums, and Lou singing in a low register without crooning or belting. His performance matches the weight of the words perfectly.

'Teach the Gifted Children' (Reed, Fonfara)

This two-chord tune is one of the most un-Lou songs in his catalog, simply because it is one of the rare times he considers the idea of progeny. Perhaps this was one of the many new possibilities that occurred to Lou and Sylvia in their newfound love. Lou never had children, and one could very cynically wonder just how a person as drastically self-preoccupied as Lou might fare in the parent department, but that is neither here nor there. Lou sounds very open and nurturing to the many necessary things that children need to be shown with love and patience. He has a list that includes sunsets, moonrise, cities, flowers, and more substantial things, like the beauty of forgetfulness, their vices and their virtues, forgiveness, mercy, and of course, music. He also mentions Al Green, requesting to be taken to the river and put in the water. The music is simple and not complex, consisting of two chords to conclude the album.

The Blue Mask (1982)

Personnel:
Lou Reed: guitar, vocals
Robert Quine: guitar
Fernando Saunders: bass guitar, backing vocals
Doane Perry: drums
Produced at: RCA Studios, New York City, by Lou Reed and Sean Fullan
Engineer: Sean Fullan
Release date: 23 February 1982
Running time: 41:00
Highest chart places: US: 169, UK: did not chart

One of the more persistent ideas in popular culture is that there are two universally acknowledged, sure-fire ways by which to excise and cauterize any essence of spark or uniqueness in a musician's work. These two ideas are 1) parenthood, and 2) sobriety. With the former, this usually results in soft, easy meditations on warmth and closeness, the sanctity of the home, being 'thankful', and, most significantly, the 'wonder of life'. With the latter, we tend to hear about the necessity of 'slowing down', taking it 'easy', and being sure to 'forgive yourself', as there are still 'plenty of tomorrows'. Both feature reduced tempos, a surplus of acoustic instrumentation, uncomplicated chords and melodies, and hummable choruses. Both are easy, gentle, and effortlessly popular, and both are very, very boring. While it could be said that the aforementioned analysis of said ideas is only really visible through the dark, blurry lenses of cynicism and mean-spiritedness, there are ample examples of this pair of concepts' justification throughout pop music to make them viable aspects of criticism.

The good news here is that, while Lou was assertively sober for *The Blue Mask*, none of the above clichés apply; really, how could anything but the height of the contrary apply to Lou? Although finished with drugs and booze, Lou's first sober album literally bleeds fire. Passions, rages, horrors; all are here as to be expected, but they burn with a new flame, an intensified concentration. There is a new seriousness here as if Lou's unclouded vision proves to him the sense that much more is on the line here, and it needs to be told in just such a way. There is nightmare aplenty here, but it is tempered with a conviction or a knowingness that distinguishes itself from all of Lou's previous work. Simultaneously, songs of love and comfort, of which there are several, have an intensity and distinctness that spare them from any kind of easy Hallmark Channel-style simplicities. A surety of purpose nourishes these songs. There's a kind of iron purity here; a sense of authenticity, now that both Lou and his art have been stripped of artifice. Make no mistake, Lou has always been a most cocksure of artists and performers, but a wholly new confidence exists here, born not so much of arrogance and posturing, but of simple, unalloyed *knowing*.

The end of his tenure with Arista finds him, curiously, back on RCA. Lou was, for once in his career, able to bask in the relative security of the consistent management afforded to him by Eric Kronfeld; so, the deal inked with his former label was, for the time being, satisfactory. All other participants were new to the fold. Co-producer and engineer Sean Fullan was an understudy of Glynn Johns and was ready to branch out on his own. Drummer Doane Perry, who worked with both Lou and Sean Fullan previously, was called in to work on this album and perhaps become a permanent member of the band. The significant gifts beheld by bass player Fernando Saunders are immediately clear after hearing just one note from his languid and lissome fretless bass. After working with such musical luminaries as Jan Hammer and John McLaughlin, he was given carte blanche by Lou to explore and decorate the sound in any way he saw fit, and he took full advantage, thus becoming a crucial component to Lou's sound for nearly the duration of his recorded career.

And then there is Robert Quine. It would be far too easy to see him as just another brilliant guitar player under Lou's employment – he was not the first, and he was not the last. Yet such an easy description is far from appropriate. Quine was most certainly brilliant, yet he was also innovative; this is important, given innovation on an electric guitar being harder and harder to find, even way back in the late 20th century. As a young law student, he would obsessively record VU concerts on tape and then, even more obsessively, study Lou's guitar to the point of rote memorization. While in New York in the 1970s, he distinguished himself as a player while working with Richard Hell and the Voidoids. To stand out as a guitar soloist among the first denizens of punk rock's hometown is no small feat; many listeners complained heartily over what they saw as antiquated overindulgence in the extended string runs of Tom Verlaine or Richard Lloyd, among others. Quine stood out, positively so.

His contributions to *The Blue Mask*, the following LP, *Legendary Hearts*, and a double live LP, *Live in Italy*, throttle the listener. There is dynamism and dexterity to his playing that clearly indicate a familiarity with the instrument, but the things he actually plays are so charged, so fraught, and so different every time – he is plugged into some other source of inspiration. A vivid freshness, coupled with an utter note-to-note unpredictability, keeps any listener engaged and curious. For *The Blue Mask*, Quine's guitar is in the left channel while Lou's is in the right, allowing the listener the ability to easily parse out who plays what. Quine has gone on record stating that he essentially forced Lou to play guitar on the album or risk losing his employment. As a result, Lou gave one of his most consistently great performances on the instrument throughout the album. Additionally, Quine tuned his guitar to D tuning, with his playing accommodating what would be a major second-tone alteration from whatever key a song might be in.

Famously, there were no rehearsals for the album; each song was completed in one or two takes and, save for Lou's second guitar on the first track, 'My House', there were no instrument overdubs of any kind. Vocals were overdubbed, with the exception of the vocals on 'The Heroine'. What we are treated to is an incredible set of recordings; a band gelling perfectly, with their leader born anew to his mission and tasks. This is one of Lou's greatest albums in his entire history.

When *The Blue Mask* was released, it garnered near-universal praise from all corners; even 'anal-retentive toe-fucker' Robert Christgau gave it an A+ in his *Village Voice* review. Yet, as even the most rudimentary study of pop music will show, critical acclaim in no way equates to hits and sales. Lou also did not tour for the album, thus relegating its sales to the still-remaining faithful. No matter, as Lou was revived and rejuvenated, and was on a roll. He would continue on with the same band, with the exception of a new drummer, on a batch of new songs that kept the machine in motion, with typically erratic results. The LP's cover, designed by Sylvia Reed, features visual references to various images from Lou's past. The central image features Mick Rock's seminal photograph from the front of the *Transformer* LP, done up in deep blue on black, recalling the black-on-black of *White Light/White Heat*. Sonically speaking, the connection between these albums is unclear, but visually, it is stunning.

'My House' (Reed)

Ice-blue, crystalline guitar chords and slippery bass guitar, untroubled by a fretted neck, open up this introductory ode to hearth and home. At first glance, it would seem that one of the easy clichés about post-trauma songwriting mentioned above was about to be checked off the list, but there is much more happening here.

> The image of the poet's in the breeze
> Canadian geese are flying above the trees
> a mist is hanging gently on the lake
> My house is very beautiful at night
> My friend and teacher occupies a spare room
> He's dead-at peace at last the wandering Jew

Amidst this newfound domestic bliss, Lou and Sylvia, via Ouija Board, come to realize that the departed spirit of Delmore Schwartz resides among them. They are both delighted with this discovery. Lou references the relationship between Stephen Daedalus and Leopold Bloom in James Joyce's *Ulysses*; the two characters' relationship is seen as an analog for their own, with Lou as Daedalus and Schwartz as Bloom. A gentle song with a comforting vibe conceals a surreal undercurrent. At 3:41, the album's only overdub enters and energizes the last two minutes of the song with a cathartic guitar crescendo.

113

'Women' (Reed)

As they say in graduate-level Humanities studies, there's a lot to 'unpack' here. Just how many layers of significance can we identify in this song? Starting with what is on the surface, there does not seem to be anything too complex at play:

I love women
I think they're great
They're a solace to the world in a terrible state
They're a blessing to the eyes
A balm to the soul
What a nightmare to have no women in the world.

Okay, not too bad, but also kind of gross, too; the adoration of woman-as-object to be collected and worshipped as a means of pleasure and release, reducing or ignoring any trace of her actual personhood: 'How can I be sexist?? I LOVE women!!!' Lou, to his credit, partially addresses this conceit: 'I used to look at women in magazines/I know that it was sexist, but I was in my teens/I was very bitter, all my sex was on the sly', but he rounds this off with the score-evening, 'I couldn't keep my hands off women/And I won't till I die'.

The chorus, simple as can be, states: 'I love women/We all love women/We love women', lest there be any ambiguity whatsoever. This is all fine, but seeing as this song was used for a music video to promote the album, can this song be seen as any kind of declaration to the public, and if so, what, exactly, is being declared? This is Lou Reed we are talking about; anyone who has paid the least bit of attention to his career up to this point knows that his orientation has been anything but conventional or private, and here he is, but a few years after living a very 'out-and-proud' existence, making very firm and clear statements that would seem very much to the contrary of what we have been shown in the past. This is fine, naturally, but such an about-face, in such inscrutable terms, makes one wonder at the suggestion of subterranean motives: not only do I love my new wife, but all that business about 'gay this' and 'gay that' was just the passing phase of a drug-taking ghost from the past. In our present illuminated age, we know that sexuality is fluid, but back in the latter half of the 20th century, it was an either/or proposition, and this song can be seen as the planting of an irrevocable stake of identity in the ground of intention for the new Lou. The music, like the previous song, is ambient and uncomplicated, with all players honoring their roles.

'Underneath the Bottle' (Reed)

Lou's time in AA influences this tale of a drunkard's woe. The tempo and groove are injected with a bit of pep, as Fernando Saunders punctuates each three-chord intro with an up-octave note, warbling and shimmering as only a fretless bass could. Lou's lyrics are the complete and total picture of an alcoholic's misery and continued justification for drinking; truly, he absolutely nails this mindset with uncomplicated precision:

Oooh wheee, look at me
Looking for some sympathy
It's the same old story of a man in his search for glory
And he found it, there underneath the bottle… Seven days make a week, on two of them I sleep
I can't remember what the hell I was doin'
I got bruises on my leg from I can't remember when
I fell down some stairs I was lyin' underneath the bottle
Ooooh wheee
Son of a B
You get so down you can't get any lower
So long world you play too rough
And it's getting me all mixed up
I lost my pride and it's hidin'
There – underneath the bottle

Nothing more needs to be said on the subject, really. The songs of drinking and drunkenness on the previous album are no less effective or truth-telling, but their perspective comes from within the action – it is tempered with a mixture of revulsion and dark acceptance. 'Underneath the Bottle' is the song of one who is outside looking in; the problem is still very current, but certain differences have been achieved in the singer's vision. He is no longer bleakly gloating about what he does, but rather, looking back to gain distance from what he did, while still centered around the same concept. As simple as this distinction may sound, the two narratives are miles apart, and it is this one that creates the impression that lasts.

'The Gun' (Reed)

This is one of the songs on the album that is truly incredible, and there are more than one. Nothing in this song rises above a murmur: the singer, the instruments, or the atmosphere. Despite that, there is an intensity in this song that is astonishing to behold. Lou's strummed chords come in along with Doane Perry's cymbal bell tings. After a few bars, Fernando Saunders slides in with, perhaps, the perfect bass riff: a mixture of smeared notes and harmonics. Robert Quine balances the song with riffs that give color but never upstage. When Lou enters, he is at first unreadable: is he so nonchalant that he does not care, or can a faint sense of barely contained mania be detected? He informs us that someone has a gun; let's see what he does. Lou speak/sings as he bounces between narrator and perpetrator.

Get over there
Move slowly
I'll put a hole in your face
If you even breathe a word
Tell the lady to lie down
I want you to be sure to see this
I wouldn't want you to miss a second
Watch your wife.

This is truly chilling to hear, and it requires no stretch of the imagination to realize what is happening in the narrative. The song is almost cinematic with regard to the intensity and vividness that the listener is subjected to. There is horror, repulsion, rage, and yet the listener creates these reactions all on their own. What the band and singer create here, sonically speaking, is quite soothing to the ear. It is when one listens to what the singer is saying that the reality comes in. There is no hysteria here, no spoon-feeding of the listener. The emotional response comes from the listener surrendering to and studying the art, rather than simply remaining stationary and letting the obvious and ever-present content stimulus wash over them. This is art you work for, and the payoff is exceptional. Legend has it that there exists an alternate take in which Lou takes the lyrics to an extreme of sorts, far outstripping what is contained herein. In a rare act of discretion, Lou chose this version for the master. The alternate version has not yet been released.

'The Blue Mask' (Reed)

This is the song. THE song. For context, let's play a bit of make-pretend, and imagine that 'Lou Reed' was just some guy who wrote songs and played guitar in New York, and managed to snare himself a recording contract around 1981. His first and only album, *The Blue Mask,* came out in 1982, and after zero sales, he was dropped from his label and his contract was considered a tax write-off. In the parallel universe that this folly occurs in, the title track of his sole album, 'The Blue Mask', in and of itself, places him squarely and irrevocably in Cooperstown, so to speak.

This song is just fucking incredible. Where to begin? Robert Quine's screaming single-coil feedback starts the tune, and Lou follows with feedback, matched by Doane Perry's rumbling toms and punishing double-bass thrusts. Chaos starts the tune, as it shall reign. After rigorous jabs and stabs, at 1:15, the groove sets in, driven and buoyed by the rawness of what has already been heard. Lou sings as a being aflame. Your author has chosen not to include any lyrics from the song, as the only way to do the song justice would be to reproduce the song in total, and that would be cheating, as your author would strongly recommend direct primary research of your own.

As a side note, in 1991, *Between Thought And Expression*, a collection of selected lyrics by Lou was published, with some of the lyrical selections offering Lou's comments in the footnotes. For 'The Blue Mask', the corresponding notes simply say 'Self-Portrait'. Is this to be believed? Are all the horrors and disgraces visited upon the protagonist in the song to be considered as reflections of the self? Lou suffered terrible anxiety as early as his grade school days in Brooklyn, and by the time of his adolescence on Long Island, the script had already been written. Self-hatred and alienation, both inwardly directed as well as outwardly projected, rode shotgun with Lou for his entire life – can any of us relate? The degradations on display here, one after another, far surpass what is commonly seen in popular music as personal exorcism. The hatred, cruelty, filth, violence, obsession, ecstasy, transformation, subjugation, surrender, declaration, acknowledgment, and fire here are expertly served and honored.

The band of musicians on hand speaks a perfect language in connection with the rigorous language Lou has laid down, and he ends the song with one of his typically inscrutable guitar solos – the kind Bob Quine had to badger him into playing. This song is incredible. A whole book could be written about just this song, but we have more to discuss…

'Average Guy' (Reed)

Side two of the LP begins with the album's closest swing at anything that could be considered 'pop' music, or at the very least, single material. Lou revives a bit of his 'dramatic voice' from the last few albums, but just a bit. His concerns here are of the pedestrian, the lumpen and the rank and file:

I worry about money and taxes and such
I worry that my liver's big and it hurts to the touch
I worry about my health and bowels
And the crime waves in the street
I'm really just your average guy
Trying to stand on his own two feet.

Middle age has come calling with a vengeance if we are to believe Lou's list of everyday concerns. The music is up and uncomplicated, in unison with the lyrical content – it is the lightest song on the album. Of the few versions of the song recorded during the sessions, there is one that was deemed even more 'commercial' than the released version. Lou specifically chose this version for the LP on account of its lack of commercial sheen.

'The Heroine' (Reed)

Lou and his guitar are the sole players for this live-in-the-studio song. It's almost folk music, to be sure. What Lou sings of is a puzzle. A ship is tossed about on a tempestuous sea. The crew have gone feral in their fear and rage, and only the heroine can put things right. Yet, despite her 'virgin white dress', and an apparent 'baby in his box', her efforts are for naught, as the ship continues to be thrown about on the water and all they can do is wait. It is no great stretch to see this as a metaphor, but a metaphor for what? The Heroine, the crew, the baby in his box, the sea: what do they represent? Without straining too hard, Sylvia could be seen as the heroine, while Lou and his interpersonal difficulties can be seen as the sea. The crew is perhaps Lou's negative and destructive impulses writ large, and the baby in his box is… perhaps the aspects of Lou that are very aware of the need for Sylvia and all she brings to him. Sometimes the baby must wait, as the sea is momentarily stormy, or the crew is rowdy and raucous. Love, successful and real love, is most certainly a long trip.

> And where's the heroine
> To fire off the gun
> To calm the raging seas
> And let herself be seized by
> The baby in the box
> He thinks the door is locked
> The woman has the keys
> But there's no moment she can seize
> Here's to the heroine
> Who transcends all the men
> Who are locked inside the box
> Will the lady let them out

This could, very simply, be just another tired old tale of how a man is nothing without the love of a good woman to help him realize his full self. Even more curiously, in *Between Thought and Expression*, this song is printed on the page opposite to 'The Day John Kennedy Died'. While not every song in the book has an addendum, the one that appears for 'The Heroine' cryptically reads: 'Jackie Kennedy trying to claw her way out of that car'. So, who knows? Is our beloved Jackie O. the heroine? Only Lou knows, and he's not telling.

'Waves of Fear' (Reed)
Fretless bass fifths begin this astute musical reading of the interior of an anxiety attack. This is another of the album's standout tracks. Lou screams off the symptoms of his terror and revulsion with the renewed integrity that his voice has discovered and applied to this album. We hear of a soul locked in rigid abhorrence, and the terror is omnipresent and immobile:

> Waves of fear
> Squat on the floor
> Looking for some pill, the liquor is gone
> Blood drips from my nose, I can barely breathe
> Waves of fear I'm too scared to leave.

What is described in this song is a full-blown psychotic episode, and anyone who has ever had their central nervous system turn on them can relate. The band thunders along with strength. The singing stops at 2:21, and at this point, Robert Quine plays what has to be the most nervous guitar solo in music history. Each note barely holds on, barely has the ability to offer itself to the ear, yet it is crucial, dynamic and absolutely essential to the song. No other guitar work will do; this is Quine's specialty, and it roars on for almost another two minutes. The guitar solo works in perfect unity with the lyrics, with everyone else admirably reporting for duty.

Once again, *Between Thought and Expression* features an addendum for this track that is telling. The songs from *The Blue Mask* tend to have the most unique and revelatory end notes: 'I was now seeing a world-famous Dr. Feelgood, who administered to various Heads of State. I wondered if they were in the same shape I was in'. This is indeed curious; was this Dr. Feelgood an aspect of Lou's rehab struggle, or was this from an experience prior to sobriety? Are the events in the song telling of a specific event, or are they an amalgamation of the illness of detox? Perhaps they are all of the above but make no mistake: there is an unassailable authenticity to this song. The singer speaks of an experience lived.

'The Day John Kennedy Died' (Reed)
For Americans of a certain generation, the assassination of John F. Kennedy serves as a time when conscious reality shattered irrevocably. This song is Lou's take on that fateful day. While Lou could be seen as one who avoids easy sympathy, it is a quiet song for a contemplative moment.

> I dreamed I was the President of these United States
> I dreamed that I was young and smart and it was not a waste
> I dreamed that there was a point to life and it was not a waste
> I dreamed that I could somehow comprehend that someone
> Shot him in the face
> Oh, the day John Kennedy died.

Many Americans simply could not comprehend how such a tragedy could happen. The assassination provided, and continues to provide, a seismic shift in how politics, the world, and, really, life are seen in its aftermath. This song is Lou's own story of his place in that aftermath. Fernando Saunders elevates the song with his heavenly harmony vocals in the chorus.

'Heavenly Arms' (Reed)
The album finishes with an unvarnished tribute to his new wife, Sylvia. Lou spares no expense drumming up the romantic energy, even if the lyrics are a bit twee in spots. The band glides through the emotional lifts and crescendos to match the singer's obvious devotion to the subject. It is a fitting end to the

album that showcases the new Lou, featuring a celebration of one of the key catalysts of this reborn artist and his energy to keep on.

Legendary Hearts (1983)

Personnel:
Lou Reed: vocals, guitar
Robert Quine: guitar
Fred Maher: drums
Fernando Saunders: bass guitar
Produced at: RCA Studios, New York City, by Lou Reed
Engineer: Corky Stasiak
Assistant Engineer: Jim Crotty
Release date: March 1983
Running time: 38:10
Highest chart places: US: 159, UK: did not chart

As there was no tour for *The Blue Mask*, things were kept apace, and the band was back in the studio in late 1982 with new drummer, Fred Maher. A talented and active NYC musician and scenester, he was the perfect mix of skill and style, and he would continue to work with Lou throughout the decade as both drummer and producer. Similar themes are explored from the previous album, but that tends to be where the similarities stay.

The album was devoted to Sylvia in its entirety, and while she also designed the cover, aspects of the ups and downs of their marriage, presumably, appear throughout. Similar themes of the struggle for sobriety, maintaining marital bliss, or at least peace, as well as larger fears and angers, are also present, just like the last album, but a certain zest is missing. Additionally, unlike the last album, there was little unity and musical and interpersonal harmony during these sessions. The cracks in the firmament appeared between Lou and his guitar player, Robert Quine. While thoroughly juiced by the vigorous praise that was lavished on *The Blue Mask,* Lou became suspicious and ultimately jealous of the fully justified admiration that was afforded to Quine; this is not atypical, as even the most cursory glance at Lou's career will see a power struggle between Lou and his ace guitar player *du jour* as grossly predictable. As a result, Quine's presence, or lack thereof, on the album raises eyebrows, as we will see.

Repeating by now a very familiar pattern, this album garnered favorable reviews and very few sales. In this case, the reviews are puzzling, as this is just a boring album. There is evidence that things could have been much fuller and heartier, but due to the, by now, predictable in-studio tension between Lou and his bandmates – specifically, his guitar player – it was not to be. Quine is quite literally mixed out of the album, and it suffers greatly because of this. Apparently, when Quine received cassettes of what was to be the master, he smashed them into bits with a hammer, such was his consternation. This would not be the end of their work together, as a brief tour of Italy was booked after a series of obligatory Bottom Line shows. This is a good thing, because we get to hear this band firing on all cylinders on material both new and old, and the performances are incendiary.

'Legendary Hearts' (Reed)

A brief, ambient cloud passes before we are introduced to the album: its sounds, voices and flavors. This gentle, soft song addresses and bemoans the true and often exhausting challenges that exist between the participants of true love, and the fears of rarely being able to live up to the 'classic romantic' images and ideals of love that have been fostered and celebrated through the years in art, literature, cinema, etc. The sound of this song serves as a good measure of what the entire album sounds like, with variations here and there. The mix is generally flat, without a lot of width to the room, so to speak. Fernando Saunders is surprisingly restrained, and Bob Quine is nearly nonexistent, a fact that would cause much consternation at the album's completion. New drummer, Fred Maher, distinguishes himself adroitly, but he is underserved by the album's colorless sound. Lou sounds unenthused and puts in more of a recitation as opposed to the barely contained explosiveness of the previous album. This would be the template for the following songs to come.

'Don't Talk to Me About Work' (Reed)

Things pep up a bit here, due in no small part to Fred Mahar's floor tom-centric beat that most certainly recalls some of Moe Tucker's finer moments with the VU. Lou also ups the energy a bit here with his character study of the haggard office worker returning home after another self-effacing day, making clear they are unavailable for any kind of conversation or communication. This thin reading would be greatly upstaged in live performance through the years.

'Make Up My Mind' (Reed)

A slow, dirge-like tempo quietly starts this tune, and it remains a quiet, uncomplicated study of indecisiveness. Lou rolls off lines without too much trouble, and the song remains untroubled by the other participants as well. The singer returns to the phrase, 'Can't seem to make up my mind', at the end of each line, but the real issue of concern finally appears at the song's end: 'Why don't you make up your mind/about leaving me behind'. As we will be given the option to ponder, all is not easy and blissful in the not-so-newlywed life of Lou and Sylvia. As listeners, we have no idea as to the truth-to-embellishment ratio, but this is a theme that runs throughout this album.

'Martial Law' (Reed)

This is one of the LP's strongest songs, and it has to do with what the band is doing. Fernando Saunders has been given a measure of slack in his leash, and his performance has a much-needed bounce that this album lacks. Robert Quine, not yet allowed a solo, plays a riff with seismic crunch here. Lou seems determined to not break a sweat as he yawns his way through this tale of vigilante enforcement in troubled urban areas. As we will see with the aforementioned 'Don't Talk to Me About Work', this song would become an explosive workout on stage.

'The Last Shot' (Reed)

Another low-key number, with unexceptional performances throughout, but the lyrics are of a different quotient. Sobriety is a long-haul struggle, and for such a seasoned abuser as Lou, the haul's length is formidable. Here, he mentions brief glimmers of some of his more squalid addiction memories:

> See this here's where I chipped this tooth
> I shot a vein in my neck and coughed up a Quaalude
> On my last shot
> Here's a toast to all that's good and here's a toast to hate
> and here's a toast to toasting and I'm not boasting
> when I say I'm getting straight, when I say I'm getting straight

'The Last Shot' can, of course, refer to both liquor and injectable drugs. For Lou, both apply, and after each set of verses, things are quantified with, 'But when you quit, you quit/but you always wish you knew it was/your last shot'. Lou must be credited for illuminating the long, hard road that leads to sobriety; this album, despite its significant shortcomings, spells out the ugly stops and starts that one must go through in order to get better.

'Turn Out the Light' (Reed)

One of the more musically interesting songs on the album ultimately leads to little. An interesting rhythm provides a perfect synchrony between Saunders and Quine, while Lou applies a low-wattage Tom Waits blur to lyrics that do little more than celebrate the end of a generally okay day. Oddly, for a song that runs for 2:50, all action stops by 1:22; the rest is simply an instrumental run through the basic riff for the song's duration. One would think that this would be a great place for a guitar solo, yet none exist.

'Pow Wow' (Reed)

Side two of the LP starts with what would not be out of place as a John Cougar Mellencamp deep-album cut. Completely uninteresting music lets Lou lackadaisically ponder on cultural assimilation and integration without too much detail. The chorus, 'I want to dance with you', would seem to suggest such a thing as the height of disparate cultural coalescence:

> When your people first moved to our block
> Our ancestors met with cultural shock
> Two different monkeys from two different trees
> Come on let's stop our fightin'
> And come dance with me

This sums it up as artfully as this yawn of a track will allow. Again, an interesting Bob Quine guitar solo would do wonders here, but once again, there are none. Listening to this track, it is not hard to see how bands such as R.E.M. or 10,000 Maniacs would experience great commercial ascension by the decade's end.

'Betrayed' (Reed)

Dreary, meandering music obscures what is, lyrically, quite an exposition. The age-old adage of 'Nobody can fuck you up in the head better than your own parents', is explored with intelligence and sensitivity here. The singer laments another vicious fight with his lover and is vexed by the sense that, while she is indeed angry with him, she is ultimately plagued by her relationship with her father and the things her father did to her – either physical, emotional, or both – as she was growing up. On the surface, the singer's claim could be seen as gaslighting: 'you're not *really* angry with me; it's *Daddy* whom you *really* hate'. A closer study of the lyrics pivots away from this idea:

> Justice taught her competence – her mother was like steel
> Her cousins, they're all convicts
> She alone rose above that wheel
> But a motorcyclist no matter how good
> Is slave to the oncoming truck
> And the poison of her father was her most pitiless luck ... Three of us lie in this bed, night of infamy.
> One of us lies on our back, her father's in her head
> And quick she turns, and slaps my face
> And with her eyes wide open she screams
> I hate you, I hate you, I hate you
> But she's looking right past me

The title of the song is, of course, 'Betrayed' – who, exactly, is betrayed here? The woman, by her own father? The singer seems to think that it is he who has been betrayed, 'by the one who says she loves you/by the one who says she needs you/above all other men'. Is this a deep conflict of allegiance between the lover and the father that the woman must settle for in order to preserve the relationship? A tall order, to be sure. As with Lou, complicated, damaging ideas are explored with clear and vivid language that distinguishes humanity among the ruins.

'Bottoming Out' (Reed)

In *Between Thought and Expression*, Lou annotates this track with 'This is an AA term as well as a motorcycle expression. In both cases, it means what it sounds like'. The song details someone feeling their worst, hazardously speeding off on a motorcycle as a means by which he hopes not to accelerate an already vicious quarrel. Rage is at the forefront here; rage that causes him to battle with his wife, rage that causes him to continue to drink, rage that causes him to make unsafe choices on his beloved bike:

> I'm tearing down Rte. 80 East
> The sun's on my right side
> I'm drunk but my vision's good
> And I think of my child bride
> And on the left in shadows I see
> Something that makes me laugh
> I aim that bike at that fat pothole beyond that underpass
> Bottoming out

It is this rage that makes existing with a loved one so fractious. It is this rage that brings one back to the bottle despite complete awareness of its potentially fatal consequences. It is this rage that makes someone take risks in an already expansively vulnerable situation. Lou's performance has a bit more brass to it here. He sings with strength and guts. Fernando Saunders has been given a bit more to play with as well. Yet again, there is almost one minute of 'dead air' as the singing stops and the band chunders on before a fifteen-second fade out. Wherefore art thou, Bob Quine?

'Home of the Brave' (Reed)

All of the songs on *Legendary Hearts* barely clock in past three minutes, with the exception of 'Home of the Brave', which wraps up at six minutes and 50 seconds, suggesting something of a centerpiece or opus. This discernment is left up to the listener. Another mournful, crawling tempo sets the mood, with Fred Maher keeping things expertly steady and punctual. Lou seems to want to spare a thought for the luckless and the suffering. He mentions the fate of his college roommate, Lincoln Sawdos, who attempted suicide by jumping in front of a train, only to permanently disable himself. The chorus states, 'Here's to the home of the brave/Here's to the life that's not saved', once again seeking to acknowledge those who happen to miss the fickle gaze of good fortune and get beaten down by life.

> The stars are hiding in their clouds
> The streetlights are too bright
> A man's kicking a woman who's clutching his leg tight
> And I think suddenly of you and blink my eyes in fright
> And rush off to the home of the brave.

This 'home of the brave' can mean any number of things; while it has always been used as a descriptive term for The United States, in the above lines, it seems to represent the place the singer returns to after being frightened by his thoughts or deeds. The love and security awaiting him in this 'home' perhaps give him the bravery required of all persons to face yet another day – a challenge that seems most acute when we are at our weakest. Musically, there is little on display here, save for a guitar solo at three minutes in. Robert Quine plays a tasteful and understated solo that never strays from the song, while, at the same time, elevating things most subtly. Despite this, the plodding nature of the song wears, and it comes off, as difficult as this is to say, a bit Grateful Dead-ish. If the tempo were not so funereal, it would be a much shorter and, perhaps, more effective song.

'Rooftop Garden' (Reed)
The album ends on an upbeat note, celebrating the quiet joys of companionship. A quiet, folk-like groove strums along as Lou recounts the simple pleasures he and Sylvia share in their urban idyll. While Lou and Sylvia had their rural retreat in New Jersey, they also kept a Manhattan townhouse, where this song presumably takes place. This track can be seen as little more than a celebration of bourgeois luxury, high above the rabble, on a lovely day. Yet it is important to have a song that celebrates those rare moments of wedded bliss at the end of an album that explores, if not practically revels in, the darker, harder sides of partnership. The music never dares to venture beyond the functional.

Live in Italy (1984)

Personnel:
Lou Reed: vocals, guitar
Fred Maher: drums
Robert Quine: guitar
Fernando Saunders: bass guitar
Recorded: Arena di Verona, 7 September 1983, and Stadio Olympico Rome, 10 September 1983
Engineer: Piero Mannucci
Release date: January 1984
Running time: 75:19
Highest chart places: did not chart

Touring for *Legendary Hearts* was by no means extensive. Following the by-now-expected series of shows at The Bottom Line in February and early March, Lou was dormant. RCA Italy contacted him with the idea of a live album. As a result, a series of dates were put together for Italy in September. Lou's popularity and influence were still formidable on the continent, and in Italy, he would be playing stadiums. In Howard Sounes' *The Life of Lou Reed: Notes From the Velvet Underground,* Fred Maher suggests that the tour was little more than R and R for Lou and his wife: 'He had set up what I would call a luxury tour. It was basically an Italian vacation for him and Sylvia'. The paucity of dates on the tour would lend credence to this idea, but it is of little matter. The double-live LP that resulted is a *tour de force* for this remarkable quartet. Chock full of VU chestnuts, apparently at Robert Quine's insistence, there are also songs from the two previous LPs that get their full sonic flourishment here on stage in front of a full stadium of rabid fans. The entire 75 minutes are punishing in their accuracy and intensity. Curiously, when the LP was released in early 1984, it was only available in Europe, the UK and Japan. It was not reissued internationally for another eleven years. It was the Italian office of RCA who solicited the recording, but a satisfactory reason for the album's exclusivity has never surfaced.The fact that this album had a limited release has caused it to be overlooked in Lou's catalog, yet it is one of his best, certainly as a live album, and this is for an artist with plenty of live albums. Lou's strength, focus, and engagement cannot be overstated. This is a sober artist who knows he has a great deal more to say and do, especially on stage, and revels in the energy he has by which to do so. After this very brief trip to Italy, it was back home and back to work, as there was plenty of work, both clean and dirty, to attend to.

'Sweet Jane' (Reed)
Following a brief introduction in Italian and a surge of crowd noise, Fred Maher counts out two clicks of his sticks to launch this seasoned opener. As

listeners, we are at once shown the sonic characteristics of the recording –
and they are good. The live sound is strong and propulsive, the instruments
are all clear and balanced accordingly, and the crowd, large as it is, is present
just enough to give a sense of scale without overpowering or suggesting post-
recording tinkering. Lou is actively engaged in his tale, Fernando Saunders
basks in the rubbery nimbleness that is his calling card, and Fred Mahar
drives things forward with a new and contemporary flair. His fills and riffs
are crisp and vivid; this is a 1980s drummer in a 1980s band. There are no
lumbering, pillow-fluffing-down-a-tumbling-hillside 1970s drum runs here.
Maher cracks and snaps with a fresh, youthful authority. Quine's crystalline
Strat is in the right speaker, while Lou is in the left, and throughout the
proceedings, they both kick up a lot of shit. This version of the classic song
is up and energized but does not overstep its role as show opener. It's a great
beginning, but it is only the beginning.

'I'm Waiting For My Man' (Reed)
Like the previous song, we listeners have been graced with many versions
over the years. Some are mournful, some are laconic, some are enraged, some
are playful and some are perfunctory. This version rips and rocks as only this
band could do. If there was any doubt about this band's ability in the wake
of such remarkable ensembles as The Everyman Band or the Hunter/Wagner
consortium, this live testament puts such concerns squarely to bed. Quine
somehow creates a guitar triumvirate of Sterling Morrison, Steve Hunter,
and himself, all the while adeptly dodging his singer's active and engaged
performance. He squeezes off two sneering, snarling solos that put a risk to
his dental health, as he bites off glaciers of raw ice. The first of these is at
1:44, and he leaps into it with a greasy slur. His second burst is at the end,
where Lou instructs him to 'Walk it home'. His riffs are pure rock 'n' roll, but
he moves from thought to thought with such unpredictability; you may have
heard each of these riffs before, but have you heard them together in this way
before?

'Martial Law' (Reed)
This is the full realization of this song; its essence was only hinted at in the
studio. If no other performance from *Live in Italy* were to be considered, this
would be the one to represent the entire album. This is a monster. Credit
once again must be given to Fred Maher; the energy positively bleeds from
the stage and speakers, yet his focus keeps things so firmly in the pocket,
that the tempo is engraved in granite, regardless of how hot the action is.
Fernando Saunders' crucial bass riff at the end of each third verse is ever
present, and Quine, already gifted with a flesh-crawling riff in the song's
initial composition, spits shards in between Lou's lines and gets a rigorous
workout at the song's end. There is not much else to be said about this song.
It must be listened to – loud!

'Satellite of Love' (Reed)

As we have seen in the past, this is a difficult one to pull off on stage. Trying
to convey the weightlessness of the studio version is a tough prospect in
person. Here, a slow and easy tempo starts us off, with each voice coming
in on its own gentle accord – it is truly almost a ballad. Lou steps into the
first verse to audible applause. Fred Mahar distinguishes each section with
reassuring stick clicks, and things move effortlessly. Quine gets in a fine solo
after the 'Harry, Mark, and John' section, following Lou's declaration of, 'This
is what I said ...' The ending vamp ups the energy and tempo appropriately,
and Lou vigorously leads us to the song's conclusion. Four tunes in, it is clear
that his level of focus and engagement is direct and consistent. Make no
mistake, this is music that is sober, severe, and surefooted. There is energy to
spare, and it comes from a real place.

'Kill Your Sons' (Reed)

Side two of the two-LP set begins with a revised epic from the chemically
enhanced days of the past decade. The hazy, quaalude-and-wine vibe of the
studio version has been replaced with a relentless mid-tempo thrust, courtesy
of Fred Maher, who is brutal here. Lou once again steers the ship with force,
and if this was not clear, he serves up a blistering solo at 3:04 that lasts the
song's duration to 5:43. Truthfully, it has been a while since Lou has given
such a naked, unshielded guitar spurt on record; there have been tastes and
flirtations here and there, but this is two-and-a-half minutes of raw not giving
a fuck. Truth be told, it is just a bit higher in the mix than anything Quine
does, but by this point, that is to be expected. The whole band pile-drives this
performance home to rapturous applause.

One point of interest here is a gender switch in the lyrics. When Lou gets
to the section of how his sister has gotten married and lives on Long Island,
what used to be an indictment of her husband, 'he's big and he's fat, and he
doesn't even have a brain', has been switched to '*she's* big and *she's* fat', etc. Is
this just an easy reflexive slip in the heat of performance, or is there a greater
taking of account here? Ask Lou.

'Betrayed' (Reed)

One of the more lyrically substantial songs from *Legendary Hearts* gets an
onstage run-through here. It is a fine, if ineffectual performance, with Lou,
once again making a committed showing to his delivery. Quine has a liquid,
jagged solo that is boosted and bolstered by Saunders' busy, warbling bass.

'Sally Can't Dance' (Reed)

It would seem that without the bouncy clavinet, white-hot brass, and wailing
vocalists, this song would lose a great deal in performance, especially with
regard to the truly rancid funk of the studio recording. Not true. There is funk
aplenty, but it is a tougher, more menacing funk, and the mellow blur of the

original version has been replaced with a bracing sheen. The tempo has been given just a bit of a bump, and all moving parts synchronize. Robert Quine sprays the room with a blistering wall of riffing in the middle of the song, while Lou maintains yet another ferocious, focused vocal performance.

'Waves of Fear' (Reed)
Another crusher. After the bass intro, the full band slams you like a tsunami of nails. Lou's vocals lack the hysteria of the studio version, replaced with a studied firmness. Fred Maher flails about with uncharacteristic abandon, and Robert Quine positively soars throughout. The accompanying riffs from the studio version stand out in fresh ways, and his avant-garde guitar solo at the end of the song, which lasts for a glorious, agonizing minute and fifteen seconds, is unequivocally impossible.

'Average Guy' (Reed)
Another tune from *The Blue Mask,* this one from the lighter side of a very heavy, emotional album. The band strolls through this uncomplicated song with ease and stride. Lou's vocal lacks some of the performative fret and worry of the original, but he is no less commanding nor convincing. Robert Quine ends the song with an understated solo that makes fine use of the Stratocaster's tonal spectrum.

'White Light/White Heat' (Reed)
Beginning side three, it is clear that the second of the two LPs that make up this set will be a walk down memory lane. It would have been nice to hear more material from the last two LPs, seeing as this was the material that this band made their own, but what remains here is of fine substance. As we have seen, the original of this song is not only impossible but also pointless to reproduce perfectly. As a result, the versions we get, and there have been a few, take on a presence of their own. Following Fred Maher's ever-present stick clicks, this one barrels out of the gate and does not let up. Maher and Fernando Saunders are joined in rigid, inscrutable lockstep, while Lou and Quine hammer away at bone-shattering power chords and Lou barks out the words, actually getting at least two-thirds of them out. The two guitars have been reversed in their stereo separation, so Quine's solo comes screaming in on the left this time – and scream it does. You can imagine a young Quine from fifteen years previous following the VU from performance to performance, taping their shows, and obsessively studying every note Lou played. His homework gets its rightful acknowledgment here.

'Some Kinda Love/Sister Ray' (Reed, Cale, Morrison, Tucker)
Clocking in at 15:30, it's time for the big concert jam. This starts with one of Lou's greatest songs ever from 'the gray album' – the third VU LP. On that version, percussion is relegated to one cowbell, while guitars strum and the

singer sings. It is not the softest song on the album, but on an already very soft album, it is a soft song that fits in with the rest. Here, in front of a full stadium crowd, it gets a necessary makeover.

Starting with a floor tom-centered beat that is perfectly merged with Fernando Saunders' 23rd-century funk riff on bass, the guitars find their way in and do their updated Lou/Sterling dialog. Both guitars are lithe and slippery, and the clapping crowd eats up every note. The vocals come in just when they should. At 2:32, Lou again joins Quine and they meander about one another in dual guitar declaration. By 6:10, all the verses have been dispersed, and the tempo begins to rise, taking us elsewhere. At 6:49, Lou first tells us about 'Duck and Sally inside', and we are at our next destination. The band vigorously pumps along while Lou spits out the words haphazardly, taking a moment now and then to allow Quine to kick the shit out of his guitar, and then do the same himself. At 9:42, Maher switches over to exclusively a floor tom thump, giving the sound a bit of breathing room. The audience can be heard clapping in tempo, far from bored by this extended workout. At 10:36, Lou hits the mic again to tell us that 'Rosie's got a new piece', with Quine answering back with some of the foulest language a guitar can utter. At 12:00, the tempo hits the ceiling with no looking back, Lou and Quine disrespecting their instruments with authority. Saunders and Maher never once break from the groove or each other; true rhythmic machinery that keeps the car on the rails. This goes until 15:10, where things are finally allowed to go over the top and end in aural cataclysm. The audience roars appropriately.

Perhaps the greatest risk of choosing to press the 'big concert moment' to record is the almost inevitable loss of translation that can occur between experience and recollection. What may have been 'heavy' or 'far out' in person can often sag and wilt on record due to the missing spontaneity and atmosphere of the performative moment. For this quarter-hour medley, the energy never lets up, the fire never cools, and the diligent listener will be rewarded with a searing performance.

'Walk on the Wild Side' (Reed)

The fourth and final side of the set features some 'greatest hits' of a sort. This song, too, is especially challenging to keep aloft onstage due to atmosphere being such a crucial component. Fernando Saunders launches, propels, and steers the song with his joyous fretless bass. He is able to gracefully occupy both of Herbie Flowers' original competing lines, while also adding an essence that is unmistakably his. Lou and Quine saw away on rhythmic chords that suggest the Richards/Jones guitar duo at their most limber. As might be expected, the tempo is brisk, but it does no harm. Lou follows the pattern of energized engagement he has established early on with this record as he goes through the song's cast of characters. Quine finishes things off with a very busy, tuneful solo. Hardly an essential reading, but this particular band cannot seem to flop.

'Heroin' (Reed)

The last two songs of the album are both powerhouses. As we have seen, 'Heroin', in essence, has to be reinvented to come off onstage; each band is tasked with its own interpretation and endgame. This is not the banana album version, the *1969 Live* version, or the *Rock 'n' Roll Animal* version. This version has plenty of polish, as this is a very polished band, but its intensity and drive are singular. After a few opening chords, Lou steps to the mic to begin 'I ... don't know...', to rapturous stadium applause. They know what they're in for. It starts very slow and almost folk rock-like, but that won't last. As the heat and the tempo rise and fall and the band go through the changes, Fred Maher never once loses focus or intent. He knows precisely when to lean on and let off, with Fernando Saunders following clearly and boldly. Robert Quine fills every area with stirring tension, while Lou has to shout himself hoarse in some sections just to stay in the saddle and keep riding with the raw force emanating from the stage. He means it. The band has the music, the mood and the massive crowd in the palm of their hand – and everybody knows it. During the final vamp, Quine plays a solo so harsh and jagged that it rivals his own vastly unique standards.

'Rock & Roll' (Reed)

While we do not know for sure if the track listing follows the order of songs, in either performance, from which these recordings were taken, this is always the perfect show closer, and here it runs at about hyper speed. There is a brief clanging of instruments before Maher clicks it off, which would suggest an encore, but it's anyone's guess. This is six minutes of blistering, blast furnace rock 'n' roll, and it does not let up. Lou roars his tale of redemption at the hands of a New York radio station like a being possessed, and he never loses a step. Once again, as if it could be any other way, his and Quine's guitars are gripped in thrashing clockwork, with Saunders so tight on the beat that he must play bass in his sleep. In the second part of the song, '... And it was alright...', Lou throws in a few lines from Stevie Wonder's 'Uptight' before launching off on one of the best solos of the two-album set. Things crash and smash with appropriate fanfare, some muddled thanks are heard from the stage and it's over – but what an ending. Use caution while driving; you might lose sight of the road.

New Sensations (1984)

Personnel:

Lou Reed: vocals, lead and rhythm guitar

Fernando Saunders: electric and string bass, backing vocals, rhythm guitar on 'My Red Joystick' and 'My Friend George'

Fred Maher: drums

Peter Wood: piano, synthesizers, accordion

Lakshminarayana Shankar: electric violin

Michael Brecker: tenor saxophone

Randy Brecker: trumpet

Jon Faddis: trumpet

Tom Malone: trombone, horn arrangement

Jocelyn Brown: backing vocals

Rory Dodd: backing vocals

Connie Harvey: backing vocals

Eric Troyer: backing vocals

Produced at: Skyline Studios, New York City, by John Jansen and Lou Reed

Engineers: Dan Nash and Roger Moutenot

Release Date: April 1984

Running time: 42:24

Highest chart places: US: 56, UK: 92

'The 80s' are here, sonically speaking. Any 'survivors' from the 60s/70s who were still cranking it out, had to, at some point, adjust to the new aural terrain now afforded to them through digital technology and the ever-expanding studio capabilities of the day, not to mention the various requirements and proclivities in the ever-shifting sands of pop commerce. Some artists, like Neil Young, went full bore, creating one of the most expansive and divisive albums in his career, *Trans,* and planting the seeds for his new label head, David Geffen, to actually sue him for creating records that were 'intentionally un-Neil Young-like'. Others, like Bob Dylan, treaded a bit more lightly; his *Empire Burlesque,* while never a fan favorite, contained decent, if unremarkable tunes amidst a wash of contemporary sonic glow. Leonard Cohen, who released only two albums in the decade, was able to wrap his significant skills around the contemporary design very effectively, particularly with *I'm Your Man.* So, where does that leave Lou and his *New Sensations*? Being his fourth album of the decade and the first without his crack quartet of the previous two, there are new things here. As soon as one drops the needle on the record (or presses the appropriate button on their device), the aural distinctions are clear. Synthesizers plump and bolster things, the drums are era-appropriately gated and triggered to sound machine-like, Lou's guitar is enveloped in effect-pedal chorus, and digital reverb rules the day. While these noticeable aspects are not extreme or exaggerated to the ear upon listening, they do make Lou sound *different,* especially for Lou.

As seen above, the band has been altered and expanded. Both Fred Maher and Fernando Saunders remain to represent the bottom end, and they have been joined by the Brecker brothers on horns, along with other such brass luminaires as Jon Faddis and Tom Malone. Keyboards are exclusively handled by Peter Wood, and a quartet of backing vocalists is on hand as well. Most conspicuous in his absence is Robert Quine. Lou has stated that at this time, due to his increased and expanded consciousness and energy as a result of his sobriety, he was in a place to have the ability to pay due diligence to his instrument, and as a result, wanted to do all the guitar by himself. The accuracy of this may be more complex. During initial rehearsals, Quine was strumming about, and Lou, being quite impressed with what he was hearing, used Quine's riff for 'I Love You, Suzanne', without giving Quine any kind of authorial credit. This, combined with his greatly reduced presence on *Legendary Hearts*, was a real issue for Quine. As far as who instigated the departure, conflicting accounts persist, but even more curiously, Quine was part of the band for the ensuing 1984 tour. Predictably, even before the close of the tour, Quine had had it with Lou's shit and declared enough was enough. This, unfortunately served as the end of a brief but fruitful partnership. This was more than just a musical disagreement. Quine was known as a low-key intellect with a strong sense of 'black humor', and his pervasively negative outlook, as described by those who knew him, informed everything he did. While this kind of perspective can be most refreshing in a world full of forced, contrived, and infantile good cheer, for Lou, who was a few years deep into sobriety, marital happiness, and renewed artistic reinvigoration, he was, perhaps for the first time in his life, borrowing a page from Bing Crosby and trying to 'accentuate the positive'. This clashed head-on with Quine's way of seeing things. *New Sensations* shows very clearly Lou's new, positive lease on life, both lyrically and sonically. Despite the risk of the alienation of the faithful, who had been ever-dwindling in numbers for some time, the risk paid off, as the album returned Lou to the middle of the charts in both the US and the UK and did quite well throughout the continent.

At this time, it is important to take a brief look at the music videos Lou had created up to this point, as their broadcast clearly influenced the sales of the albums from whence they came. For *The Blue Mask*, Lou did a video for 'Women', which featured a fairly nondescript mimed band performance. For *Legendary Hearts*, Lou produced videos for the title track and 'Don't Talk to Me About Work'. Both videos feature Lou mouthing the lyrics while VHS-era video effects are swirling about him. The theatrical quotient is elevated for the two videos from *New Sensations*. The first, for 'I Love You, Suzanne', features a calm and slightly exasperated Lou being led around by a tall, spritely blonde – the 'Suzanne' in question. The Suzanne character is all sass and spirit; she knows everybody in the club where Lou is playing on stage, and many men in the club would like to capitalize on that connection. Suzanne whirls and bounces about, always with a smile on her face, and the spritz and shimmer of 80s hair and fashion abound throughout the production. Despite her flightiness, she is true to her Lou, and he to her.

The second video, for 'My Red Joystick', actually continues the theme of these unlikely lovers. A clearly disgruntled Suzanne, played by the same actor from the previous video, with the help of her supportive, energetic friends, is hastily loading random items and boxes of belongings into the back of a moving van, while Lou mimes the words to his assortment of musician and on-the-corner friends. He stays out of her way until she steps up with a box that contains clearly visible Lou Reed LPs, and he stops her to reach into the box and retrieve the same red joystick from the album's cover. Good times. Both of these last two videos received their fair share of airplay on MTV, which was by now starting to come out of its infancy. As we know, music videos became successful because they were financially successful, and even Lou Reed could reap the benefit.

'I Love You, Suzanne' (Reed)
Opening with a line from a classic by The Contours, a bright, peppy, high-end pop song about not much in particular, starts things off. The lyrics do not stray beyond declaring love for someone named Suzanne, and the sound is very loud and up. The drums are gated and soaked with treble, the bass is busy and full of notes, and the rhythm guitar is almost jangly. Lou's brief, repeated guitar solo is uncharacteristically tamed and organized; perhaps this is what was pilfered from Robert Quine. As per usual, it is this first song that gives the listener a taste of how the remainder of the album will flow. It's the 80s.

'Endlessly Jealous' (Reed)
In the exact same key as the previous song, we have another blast of canned air. Fernando Saunders has some assistance from a sequenced synthesizer bass line, and the drums are brightened to the extent of sounding like the equivalent of a solar flare. The lyrics have a bit more to offer; they give an honest portrayal of a lover's jealousy, and how this can often feed and feed off of the jealousy of their partner: 'Endlessly jealous of you/Being endlessly jealous of me/The man that you thought I could be/Turning red with jealousy'. This is followed by a bridge that details the many things the singer feels they must apologize for. It's a good era-appropriate pop/rock song, and, similar to the previous song, Lou delivers a believable, uncontrived performance.

'My Red Joystick' (Reed)
It's RnB time. Fernando Saunders helps with this concession by applying sharp rhythm guitar to his usual bass duties. Lou's lead guitar parts are very smooth and together, as well as used very sparingly to good effect. The

lyrics bounce back and forth between playing on the Biblical character of
Eve, and someone pleading with their acrimonious lover to leave them their
red joystick:

> The first bite of the apple made Eve smart
> The second bite taught her how to break men's hearts
> The third bite taught her how to strut her stuff
> But she never got to the fourth bite that says
> Enough is enough... Eve drank apple cider
> Eve brewed good apple wine
> Eve cooked up stewed apples
> Knew how to have a good time
> She came into the bedroom
> Raised her skirts up high
> She said, 'If a little knowledge is a dangerous thing, baby
> Give me a piece before I die'
> Hey Eve take a bite of my apple
> I know you think you're pretty slick
> The one thing I ask you to leave me
> Is my Red Joystick

Those searching for depth or meaning in the lyrics can go in a few different
directions. This can be read as another 'true love is a pain in the ass, yet
(almost) always worth it' tale of the ups and downs of the heart, and if the
lover has truly had enough and is leaving, the least they can do is not take
everything, both material and emotional, with them.

With another set of lenses, this can also be seen as yet another testament
to the time-honored surrender of the will and power that men, or at least
hetero men, have felt helpless to at the hands of a beautiful, willing woman.
This woman, this Eve, so knowing and adept in her wiles, knows all too
well that any schlub of a man is putty in her hands, and all he can do is
blissfully give in to her amorous undertow. Rather than sternly protest
or feebly resist, he gives in to his throbbing urges, save for one humble
request: take from me all you will, but please at least leave me with my ...
red joystick?

As the 1970s bled into the 1980s, the relatively new technology of video
games heralded the beginning of a cultural ascension that resulted in the
rise to the influential position they now have, and with this, came a new
terminology. Joystick was the unironically chosen term given to the main
tool of interface the game player uses; Lou is seen holding one, red in color,
on the album's cover. The fairly obvious phallic properties of the device, in
not only its name but also its design, allow it to be seen as a stand-in for the
singer's masculinity here; by pleading with his powerful lover to not deprive
him of it, he is asking for just a slight percentage of power to be kept for

himself. She can, and possibly will, take everything from this man, and due to the pleasure and satisfaction he receives in return, he is ok with that, though surely not overlooking any deep-seated fears and anxieties he may have over emasculation or castration. Serving as a bulwark against the loss of his actual maleness, the promise of being left with his red joystick, in the wake of intimacy or the wake of an argument, allows him to remain a man, despite any surrender of power. These male fears of a loss of gender-based identity at the hands of a strong female partner are reactionary in the extreme, but old habits, especially habits of emotional anxiety, die hard.

'Turn to Me' (Reed)
Starting with a Rolling Stones riff without a home, this rocker serves duty to Lou's new enthusiasm and positivity. After rattling off a list of problems and inconveniences, Lou concludes each stanza with the ever-hopeful, 'Remember I'm the one who loves you/You can always give me a call/Turn to me'. This is not your father's Lou Reed. Strengthened with backing singers and another measured, even-keeled solo, the sparse instrumentation keeps the motor humming warmly. There is perhaps a brief glimpse of autobiography in here as well when Lou adds a key element to his scroll of stressors: 'Your wife says maybe it's time to have a child'. This very idea will be revisited with much greater detail and vision a bit further down the line, but it is interesting to see it rear its head here.

'New Sensations' (Reed)
This is a great song. Earlier on in this book, the concept of the outlier was mentioned as a standout track that can redeem an otherwise unexceptional album. While this track is not necessarily the outlier, it is the album's flagship song. Fading in with a smooth, pseudo-*motorik* beat, bass and guitar join in, and then Lou steps forward with his ideas about New Sensations:

> I don't like guilt be it stoned or stupid
> Drunk and disorderly I ain't no cupid
> Two years ago today I was arrested on Christmas Eve
> I don't want pain, I want to walk not be carried
> I don't want to give up, I want to stay married
> I ain't no dog tied to no parked car
> New Sensations
> I want the principles of a timeless muse
> I want to eradicate my negative views
> And get rid of these people who are always on a down
> It's easy enough to tell what's wrong
> But that's not what I want to hear all night long
> Some people are like human Tuinals
> New Sensations

Strong and focused things. To change oneself, really change oneself, is a
Herculean undertaking, and the very first step is truly wanting to do so. This
can be said for any kind of change: employment, addiction, relationships,
habitat, or attitude and outlook. Lou Reed, the man, along with 'Lou Reed',
the persona, has often been noted and celebrated for his vast and storied
study of the lost and the bleak, offering glimpses and visions of the humanity
that exists within the darker corners of existence. Marriage and sobriety have
worked wonders for Lou now that he, in his early forties, is able to truly
apply himself to the changes that these choices require. At the center of it all
lies a change of attitude, a change in seeing and how one sees. This song lays
these ideas out with a purity and directness that only Lou can produce.

The second half of the song's lyrics detail a ride Lou took on his beloved
Kawasaki GPZ and the pleasurable chance encounters and circumstances
he discovers as a result. Musically, the song is exceptional in its approach to
mood and color. There is a lot of space here, and the background singers,
truly a united bunch, add greatly to the chorus. Additionally, after each
chorus, an uncredited pedal steel slips out reverbed notes of gold. Pedal steel
on a Lou Reed album might seem incongruous, but here it is perfect. The
song has a glide and momentum that strongly resembles a motorcycle's ride
through the countryside in brisk weather.

'Doin' the Things We Want To' (Reed)
The LP's second side begins with heavily chorused guitar strums. Lou begins
to tell us about seeing a recent Sam Shepard play, presumably, *Fool For Love*.
Lou describes how he was quite moved by the writing and the performance
of the play, and after each line, he repeats the song's title while L. Shankar's
violin floats in on clouds of otherworldly reverb. Lou sings and strums for 1:41
before the band crashes in with era-appropriate anthemic grandeur. Lou goes
on to forge a connection between Shepard's work and that of Martin Scorsese,
affectionately known here as 'Marty', and praises the inspiration he has often
gotten from the characters within both of these artists' works. He concludes
the song with the lines, 'I wrote this song 'cause I'd like to shake your hand/In
a way you guys are the best friends I ever had'. Strong praise, indeed. A true
Lou song in that it has no more than two chords, it has a reputation as one of
his banner compositions. Legend tells of Bob Dylan seeing Lou perform the
song in concert and being moved enough to mention to Sylvia that he wished
he had written the song himself. Upon hearing this, Lou, to no great surprise,
boisterously proclaimed Dylan to be one of the greatest toilers of songcraft,
and immediately dispatched a roadie to a record store to scarf up all the Dylan
vinyl they had in stock. Once again, strong praise, indeed.

'What Becomes a Legend Most' (Reed)
The most dramatically arranged song on the album begins with violin by L.
Shankar that sounds strangely sampled and played via digital keyboard, but

this could just be due to the crispness and precision of his playing. Lou joins him, asking questions regarding the true identity behind public praise and notoriety. His questions are directed toward a female protagonist, and this can be seen as a revisiting of the ideas from the VU's 'New Age' from fourteen years previous. Once again, the band's arrival had been delayed, and when they enter, the snare drum is gated to the point of resembling a rock striking a pane of reinforced glass. The loneliness and isolation of fame are listed, prefaced each time with a repeat of the song's title, as the band goes through some interesting and uncharacteristic chord and arrangement styles in the bridge. Oddly, Lou ends the song with: 'What becomes a legend most/When she's lying in her hotel room/What becomes a legend most/Well baby tonight it's you', raising the question of who he might actually be addressing here. One of the weaker offerings on the album.

'Fly Into the Sun' (Reed)
A curious piece of 80s pop-folk music here. Closely resembling the title of the VU leftover from his first solo LP, this song speaks of Lou's lack of fear or avoidance were he to face death. He speaks of death as a release from pain, as well as a chance to receive answers to many of life's deepest conundrums:

I would not run from the Holocaust
I would not run from the bomb
I'd welcome the chance to meet my maker
And fly into the sun ... I'd see it as an end to misery, as an end to worldly pain
I'd shine by the light of the unknown moment
To end this worldly pain... To end this mystery, answer my mystery
I'd look at this as a wonderous moment to end this mystery
Fly into the sun-fly into the sun

A relatively quiet arrangement features Lou, Saunders, Maher and the background singers to add just a whisp of gospel flavor. Not the most musically dynamic track, but the lyrics are an interesting take on mortality, especially coming from someone who has been given a second chance as a result of cleaning up their act.

'My Friend George' (Reed)
This fairly basic song begins in a way that would not sound at all out of place on a contemporary release on I.R.S. records, which saw its heyday in the mid-80s. This is another one of Lou's errant character songs where someone he might have known and admired as a kid grew up to become troubled, and in this case, homicidally violent. Despite this, Lou still considers George to be his friend and wishes him the best. This song has an air of the tall tale narrative from the folk tradition, and it certainly calls to mind previous

character studies from the past – 'Billy' from *Sally Can't Dance* comes to mind. Peter Wood's piano and synthesizer add embroideries to an otherwise bland song.

'High in the City' (Reed)

As is now painfully clear, it would not be an 80s album without a watered-down reggae-lite track, so here we have 'High in the City'. While not totally bland and cruise ship-worthy, its easy and forgettable arrangement leaves no lasting impression. The lyrics speak of a weaponized person, with their equally armed friend, desiring to go out at night, get high, flirt with danger, and make out on a park bench, all in the city. A night out on the wild side of the city lights, to be sure. Tom Malone gets an all-too-brief trombone solo to introduce the fade-out, and the background singers once again add their polish.

'Down at the Arcade' (Reed)

This cutesy-pie twelve-bar album closer is a tribute to Lou's latest pastime: the pinball and video arcade. Were it not for its tough contemporary production, it could have just as easily been a product of Shadow Morton or Don Kirshner from 20 years previous. It boasts all of the self-centered pomp of the classic hits of that bygone era. It's a fun, braggadocio way to end an album on which Lou took certain sonic and commercial chances as a means of forging new territory. By and large, these chances worked.

Mistrial (1986)

Personnel:
Lou Reed: vocals, lead guitar, rhythm guitar
Fernando Saunders: rhythm guitar on 'Tell it to Your Heart' and 'Don't Hurt a Woman', bass
guitar, synthesizer, programming, piano on 'I Remember You', percussion on 'Outside', backing vocals
Eddie Martinez: rhythm guitar on 'No Money Down', 'Don't Hurt a Woman', and 'The Original Wrapper'
Rick Bell: tenor sax on 'No Money Down'
J.T. Lewis: drums on 'Mistrial', 'Don't Hurt a Woman', and 'Tell it to Your Heart', percussion
on 'No Money Down'
Sammy Merendino: programming on 'Don't Hurt a Woman' and 'Tell it to Your Heart', percussion on 'No Money Down', 'Video Violence', and 'The Original Wrapper'
Jim Carroll: backing vocals on 'Video Violence'
Rubén Blades: backing vocals on 'I Remember You' and 'Tell it to Your Heart'
Produced at: The Power Station, Manhattan, NYC, by Lou Reed and Fernando Saunders
Mixed by: Bruce Lampcov
Release date: June 1986
Running time: 39:12
Highest chart places: US: 47, UK 69

After a truly active, high-profile year, Lou once again designed to work amongst pop convention. A 'live' drummer featured on only three out of ten tracks on the album, while the remainder feature rhythm machine programming by Fernando Saunders and Sammy Merendino. This can be seen as a very distinct tilt toward the pop conventions of the day, but following the previous album, this is not so foreign here. One of the significant differences between *Mistrial* and *New Sensations* is that this album is much more produced. This might sound odd at first glance, but there is a clear discrepancy. On *New Sensations*, the triggers are plugged in; the compressors are revved up, and off they go. With an assorted array of embellishments, like synths and backing vocals, the tracks are still very Lou Reed; that is, the sonic atmosphere is still fairly uncomplicated. On *Mistrial*, there is very little spare air; rather, the instrumentation is busy and excessive. It is just a much bigger production, a much bigger-sounding album. On some tracks, Lou is almost buried beneath the sheer sonic weight of all that is going on in the track. Whether this can be seen as a strength or a detriment rests with the listener, yet once again, Lou's presence and performance are dedicated and focused, as is the pattern of his work as a result of his sobriety. Like Captain Beefheart's two LPs for the Mercury label, *Mistrial* is the album of Lou's career that biographers and critics have the least amount of time for; it usually has the least amount of ink devoted to it. Here we shall attempt to give it its fair due.

Creating music videos with a certain degree of creative muscle worked wonders, financially speaking, for the previous album, so it happened again here. For 'No Money Down', Kevin Godley and Lol Creme, of 10cc and Godley and Creme, created a purely animatronic Lou Reed stand-in that mouths the song's lyrics before ripping itself to shreds: skin, eyes, and all. It's a great video. For 'The Original Wrapper' – because there had to be a video for 'The Original Wrapper' – a team of Hazmat suit-clad workers busily rush about the city placing various urban denizens in casket-like cardboard containers while Lou mouths the lyrics in a fedora. This video, too, shows a certain artistic cleverness indicative of the era when a music video could still be considered 'interesting'.

Lou toured extensively in 1986 with most of the players from the album. He did a few one-off gigs in 1987, and then there was a pause in his action. He wrote and produced three songs for Panamanian singer Rubén Blades' first English-language album, *Nothing but the Truth*, in 1988. As might seem painfully predictable at this point, Lou had also turned sour on his longest-standing manager Eric Kronfeld and would begin to self-manage his career with essential involvement from Sylvia, who would wholly assume the role not long thereafter. Lou would not have another album out until January 1989. He would have brand new players, a new label, new songs and his sound would once again be greatly revised.

'Mistrial' (Reed)
With plenty of strut and swagger, this generally middle-of-the-road rocker opens up the proceedings with flourish. As one of the tracks that features a live drummer, the rock 'n' roll aspect of this song is pushed to the fore. As the sole guitarist on the track, Lou is featured throughout on both lead and rhythm, and his playing is smooth and ordered. The lyrics speak of a lifetime troublemaker who had his 'first lady' at six years old, and his first drink at eight years old, etc. He now demands a 'mistrial to clear his name', for the purpose of... who knows? The chorus has plenty of attitude to catch the fleeting attention of the youth market: 'You can call Mister/You can call me Sir/But don't you point your finger at me'. Several biographers have pointed out that, technically, the use of mistrial as a legal concept is incorrect in this context, as a mistrial is typically called during a court case where there has been some sort of error in the proceedings. Here, the singer is asking his 'record' to be expunged, but this is mere pedantry.

'No Money Down' (Reed)
Programmed rhythms and shimmering sequenced synths lay the foundation for a statement on the risks that lovers take with each other, which can seem especially glaring in the light of disappointment. The three sets of verses tell of the struggles and contradictions people face both alone and together, and

the chorus ties it all together with 'You're paying a price/when there's no price to pay/Lover's trust-no money down'. Between verses, Lou's lead guitar plays riffs with Rick Bells' tenor sax to the song's benefit. A very produced piece of pop commerce.

'Outside' (Reed)

This is a percussion-centered examination of the clearly present question of whether or not to reproduce, which the listener can easily establish as a very current topic between Lou and the Mrs at the time. The track has been constructed from the ground up by Lou and Fernando Saunders, and its energy and propulsion are of a piece with the rest of the LP. Lyrically, Lou covers some interesting territory:

Outside the world's a mindless child
Outside
Outside reflects the worst of styles
Outside
Inside when you're in my arms
A mindless child is still to be born
Inside, baby, when we come inside ...
Outside they don't think they breed
Outside
Outside emotion determines need
Outside
Outside the world's a mindless child
That we could bring to life
In your arms
Inside, baby, when we come inside

There are a number of lyrical spins here. The concern of a brutal, chaotic world that exists just beyond the door is especially jarring when one considers bringing a child into the mix. It is clear in the lyrics that reproduction is something to be considered, analyzed, posited and debated, as opposed to those 'outside', who, according to the singer, breed indiscriminately, based solely on selfish emotional impulse. Additionally, the last line of each stanza, '…when we come inside', suggests internal, as opposed to external, or 'pulling out', ejaculation as it relates to potentially ensuring pregnancy. The final line of the song is 'Inside, a baby's what you want inside', which indicates fairly clearly what kinds of discussions are going on in the Reed family home.

'Don't Hurt a Woman' (Reed)

Another in a long line of Lou Reed apology songs, which gained strong prevalence during his second marriage. The second song to feature live drums by J.T. Lewis as well as rhythm guitar by both Fernando Saunders and Eddie Martinez, it also features programmed rhythms and synths by Sammy Merendino. This essentially standard ballad arrangement, with lumbering tempo, echoing percussion, and a I-VI-IV-V chord progression, would aptly serve as the background music for the inevitable teen breakup scene to any number of 80s teen dramas that seemed to be on every screen at the time. The performance serves these ideas up with a clear sense of legitimacy and honesty.

'Video Violence' (Reed)

This almost entirely programmed rocker serves as an indictment of what, at the time, was seen as shock and surprise to the now commonly accepted idea of the prevalence of images on easily accessible video, and how it quickly and easily panders to the most base within us. As a culture, we have thoroughly and unquestioningly accepted unchecked standards of violence in our entertainment without any kind of filter or control as a given, yet we are still clutching our collective pearls over any kind of meaningful depiction of sexuality; this double standard is magnified with regard to what is considered 'acceptable' for young people. This song questions and calls out our culture's tacit allowance of unchecked graphic violence in our media. The lyrics are vivid in their imagery and detail:

> Up in the morning, drinking his coffee
> Turns on the TV to some slasher movie
> Cartoon-like movie, tied up and sweaty
> Panting and screaming
> Thank you, have a nice day ...
> Our good working stiff looks a whore in the eye
> Ties her to a bed
> While he beats her black and bloody
> And then back at home
> Drinking more instant coffee
> Calls some red-neck evangelist that
> He's seen on TV and says
> The currents rage, the dawn's upon us
> This is the age of video violence

Musically, this is a very active track, with plenty of guitar riff snarl and sidewind; Lou's vocals are almost buried in the mix. For those interested, Lou is backed up by NYC poetic poseur Jim Carroll on the 'na-na-na-na-na-na' choruses. It is a very strong track in terms of lyrics, performance and production.

'Spit it Out' (Reed)

The track that begins side two of the LP is a product of Lou and Saunders exclusively; amongst the programmed beats and sequences, there is guitar aplenty, and the track has a surplus of drive. The lyrics, while fairly basic, offer an encouragement to the listeners to verbally announce their consternation in moments of strife, as opposed to tightening the lip and keeping it inside. Both the music and the lyrics are uncomplicated in their delivery and intent.

'The Original Wrapper' (Reed)

Well, it's come to this – Lou Reed 'raps'. It's not all bad, really; Lou's vocals have always treaded the line between singing and speaking. This just seems a bit more up-tempo, wedded to a most topical and timely track that is almost entirely programmed. Vocally, he does not try to sound anything other than himself. Like a lot of the hip hop at the time, his vocals reel off a laundry list of concerning social and political trends and occurrences without a great deal of detail going into any of them. A tongue-twistingly verbose section of lyrics reads:

Kick up your heels-turn the music up loud
Pick up your guitar and look out into the crowd
And say 'Don't mean to come on sanctimonious
But life's got me nervous and a little pugnacious-Lugubrious so I give a salutation
And rock on out to a beat really fabulous
Ohh poop a doo and how do you do
Hip hop gonna bop till I drop'

This is all tied up at the chorus with, 'Hey pitcher better check that batter/ Make sure the candy's in the original wrapper'. A not too terribly cringe-worthy valiant attempt at new pop trends of the time.

'Mama's Got a Lover' (Reed)

This guitar-driven character study is interesting in that it leaves the listener in want of further details from the participants. The story within is by no means riveting; Lou has done plenty of that before and since, but this could be seen as a play or television drama. 'Mama' in the song has a new lover who seems to have an impact on not just her companionship but also her employment and social station as well:

Mama's got a lover
A painter I am told
She's getting out of real estate
For the art scene down in old Soho
Mama's got a lover
He owns a gallery
She says he likes collages but
The money's in GRA-FI-TI.

So far, so good, and we get to the chorus:

> Mama's got a lover
> I met him yesterday
> She says she hopes I like him
> Maybe I'll send him a card on Father's Day.

The singer's real thoughts on the subject arrive in the last two sets of verses:

> Mama's got a lover
> He's got something to say
> He says he's into dirt and rot
> The essence of 'urban decay'
> Mama's got a lover
> I met him yesterday
> She's starting a new chapter
> I wish she was on the last page.

Good, rich family drama with a taste of culture and creativity to it, to be sure. Lou provides another of this era's measured and tamed guitar solos, and the track concludes with a nearly 40-second fade.

'I Remember You' (Reed)
Starting with and being dominated by a sunny, pure pop rhythm guitar riff, this unchallenging declaration of reminiscence puffs along with no trace of struggle or substance. The lyrics bare no detail or exception to the surface-level observations, and the music, beyond the aforementioned guitar, remains unchanged. Perhaps it is filler time.

'Tell it to Your Heart' (Reed)
With the third and final track of the LP featuring live drums from J.T. Lewis and bass from Fernando Saunders – which actually hints at his distinct style of playing – we end things with another Big Lou Ballad. The music is uncomplicated in its senior prom-like tempo and arrangement, and the sonic conventions of the day are fully represented here with torrential reverb, gated snare drum, and little breathing space. Lou details being up on his Manhattan roof at night and seeing a series of spinning lights. Unsure if he should awaken his partner, presumably Sylvia, to see them herself, he goes down to the street to pursue his strange vision, only to realize that a TV commercial is being filmed. The chorus seems unconnected to this:

> Tell it to your heart
> Please don't be afraid
> I'm the one who loves you in each and every way

Tell it to your heart
Please don't be afraid
New York City lovers
Tell it to your heart.

It's a perfectly nice enough song, but one cannot help picturing awkward, brace-toothed teens, who have been stealing glances at one another in their various high school hallways and after-school activities for the last commercial-free 75 minutes, finally holding one another close under soft lights in the gym, while the dance floor respectively clears for their one big romantic culmination at the near-90 minute mark. Not that there's anything wrong with that.

It is at this point, in a career littered with various crossroads of one kind or another, that Lou faced and negotiated yet another crossroad; a crossroad of not only great significance but one that could not be adequately observed and analyzed until within its aftermath. For the last seventeen years, Lou Reed had been busily attempting to create Lou Reed. With baggage aplenty, both personal and professional, he had sought to stand out, create, and be accepted on his own terms; terms that are both rigidly inflexible as well as haphazardly capricious. He had both applied and rejected many guises and forms as a means of establishing his own breed of artistic and commercial success, careening between both aping and rejecting many of the day's various standards, all the while trying to keep a faithful attachment to his muse. His next three albums would usher in a new kind of success and acceptance for Lou; success and acceptance of a kind he has not seen before, nor perhaps since. These three LPs, one of which being a coproduction with an erstwhile colleague of repute, will justifiably be seen as works of a quality long hinted at but not yet seen by Lou. Here, Lou would finally gain the full acceptance of 'The Academy'; the fickle and oftentimes reactionary consortium of pop culture historians and tastemakers. Additionally, while still not topping the charts, these albums would return Lou to a degree of commercial success long sought after but never grasped. It is these three albums that will set the tone and secure a place for Lou for the duration of his career, as they are only the beginning of his second chapter, which will be explored fully in the second volume of this series.

Appendix – Additional Recordings

Bataclan '72, with John Cale and Nico (2003)

While heavily bootlegged over the years, this legendary one-off performance from January 1972 in Paris finally saw a semi-official release on various labels in 2003 and beyond. There has been some discrepancy over how this *de facto* VU reunion came to be: some reports state that Lou booked the gig while working on his solo debut in London and casually invited his two erstwhile colleagues along; others state that Cale and Nico, who had just completed work on Nico's third LP, *Desertshore*, had arranged a joint show, and then decided to give their ol' pal Lou a call. Regardless, what remains is singular. The expertly recorded show, which was also filmed for French television, sees each artist taking turns at center stage, with Lou being first in line. This performance is especially significant in a number of ways. Not only was this performance a good five months before the release of *Lou Reed*, but this may also have very well been his first performance of any consequence since the final days of August 1970; in short, this moment captures him live well before he became 'Lou Reed'.

He begins the show with five songs, accompanied by Cale on either piano, viola, or acoustic guitar. Three of these songs are VU chestnuts, while the remaining two songs will soon appear on his first solo LP later in the year. With regard to his performance, he is both cordial and witty; his voice is in fine shape, and he seems committed to the occasion. When introducing 'I'm Waiting For the Man', he casually mentions that 'This is a song about copping drugs in, uh... drugs in New York', and the ensuing performance is as cool and smooth as his delivery. For 'Berlin', Cale expertly lays out the chordal intro on piano while Lou declares 'This is a new song... my Barbara Streisand song'. The performance adheres closely to the *Lou Reed* version, with Lou singing with depth and strength while Cale luxuriates the melody upon the piano keys. It's a lovely performance.

The third selection, 'The Black Angel's Death Song', may seem an odd choice, but this rare performance pays off. In Lou's introduction, he states that the song '...was termed unintelligible, and it may very well be', followed by rapturous applause that is equal parts surprise and enthusiasm. With Lou on acoustic guitar, Cale on viola and a slightly reduced tempo, the lyrics are brought to the foreground, and much of the guesswork that committed listeners to The Banana Album toiled in for several years, can be at last laid to rest. This track is one of the most frequently bootlegged cuts from this performance for this very reason. 'Wild Child', again from his forthcoming debut, sees Lou soaring into the choruses with vocal strength and poise, thoroughly at ease with his material and circumstance. At its intro, Lou banters about with the audience, declaring: 'Take a, uh, minute while Johnny gets his, uh, twelve-string... that's the name of a new movie'. At this, Cale responds, 'What?' and Lou repeats 'Johnny gets his twelve-string... he lost his legs, but he got a twelve-string', humorously riffing on the at-the-time recently released anti-war film, *Johnny Got His Gun*.

Finally, the inevitable 'Heroin' gets an outing, with Cale once again on viola, and despite its reduced arrangement, it is riveting. While tuning the viola to the guitar, Lou casually mumbles, 'OK, this song didn't get us banned'. Rich applause rises up upon Lou's utterance of those first key words: 'I... don't know...' and all effortlessly falls into place. The two players navigate all the twists and turns of this singular composition with dexterity and poise, both clearly involved in the performance. It is nice to hear Lou so consistently giving a shit. The remainder of the performance sees three Cale compositions, followed by three absolutely devastating Nico performances, accompanied by Cale, before they all join hands for 'Femme Fatale', and an encore: 'All Tomorrow's Parties'.

This is a recording that captures a number of things on the cusp: Cale, soon to become an in-house producer for Reprise Records, vastly elevating his status in the post-VU world, paving the way for his own distinct and distinguished solo career; Nico, sadly, on her way to full-blown addiction and sparse productivity, as she would release only two additional LPs in the remaining decade; and Lou, hovering right next door to becoming Lou Reed. There is a barely-there trace of almost extinct purity in these recordings. All three players have already been kicked around by The Entertainment Industry quite a bit, and there would certainly be much more to follow, but somewhere within this performance is the vague, naïvely hopeful sense that the candlelight of belief in the purity of expression has not been fully and completely snuffed yet. Give it time; that will happen, but we can't hear it here just yet.

I'm So Free: The 1971 RCA Demos (2022)

Reaching even farther back in time, this Record Store Day collection of acoustic demos, recorded under the watchful eye and ear of producer Richard Robinson, has a somewhat dubious, if not at least cynical, commercial pedigree. This collection of recordings was released without fanfare and just as quickly withdrawn from circulation as an apparent example of what is referred to as a 'copyright dump'. This term is used to describe archival releases of songs by legacy artists that record labels release to the public purely as a means of extending a soon-to-be-expired copyright on the artist's material. Typically, depending on the various laws of a certain territory, this occurs at or around the 50-year mark of an artist's extended contract. The record labels/entertainment conglomerates that possess the catalogs of Bob Dylan, The Beatles, The Rolling Stones, The Beach Boys and the Motown label, among others, have all launched various collections of demos, outtakes, or odds and ends of songs, usually without any involvement from the artist in question, as a means of locking down continued ownership without interruption. Heaven forfend such lucrative material falling prey to the public domain. While this practice can be seen as yet another lurid and gluttonous example of the loathsome stranglehold that commerce has on creativity, everything exists forever on the internet, and for committed fans, these copyright dumps can bring forth good fruit.

What we have here is a collection of seventeen songs recorded in a small Manhattan RCA studio on 27 October 1971, almost all of which have not seen previous release, save for the demo versions of 'Perfect Day' and 'Hangin' Around' that appeared as bonus tracks on the 2002 edition of *Transformer*. Lou and his guitar, in what David Fricke's liner notes detail as the very first recording of Lou Reed as a post-VU solo artist, are in fine form, with energy, fresh playing and singing and good humor to spare. Despite the exclusivity of these tracks, there is nothing freakishly new here; any seasoned listener can easily trace each song's lineage to either the last year of Lou's involvement with the VU or his first two solo LPs, but there are a few surprises. 'Love Makes You Feel' in its acoustic form still contains space for the 'prog-lite' rave-up at its conclusion on the debut LP, again evidenced by Lou declaring '... sounds like this', before turning up the drive on his guitar strumming, while 'Going Down' is invested with much more feeling in its unaccompanied folk-style version as opposed to its tiresome, sluggish official LP version. There is a bit of good-natured banter at the start of 'Ocean', which remains most closely connected to the *Lou Reed* version, but there is not a great deal of studio chatter on display on the whole, save for Lou occasionally announcing 'Fade' to indicate a song's aural conclusion, with the recording appropriately following suit.

While most of the songs herein are true to form, with mild lyrical variations here and there, it is the demo of 'Kill Your Sons' that is most revelatory. When it appeared on *Sally Can't Dance* in 1974, it was a clear and brutal indictment of the treatment that troubled young men could count on at the hands of the psychiatric community. Here, it is a very era-appropriate railing against what, at the time, was referred to as the generation gap. The chords and 75% of the chorus are the same; the rest of the lyrics are wholly different. A sample from the first stanza:

All your drunken congressmen
Are gettin' out the vote
By shipping out the youngest
to war in tax-paid boats
And filling up the jails with youth
who will not drink their swill
You've broken all our hearts
but you cannot break our will
You know you're gonna'
Kill your sons
You know you're gonna' hafta' kill
Kill all of your sons
You know you're gonna' kill

kill all of your sons
Until they
Reclaim the land

The verses that follow detail various digs and discussions between the 'youth' and the 'aged' that, again, are very much of their time. Lou sings this with a powerful delivery that could place him among the many second-tier Baezes and Ochs that were seemingly popping up everywhere, guitars in hand, at the time of this recording. On the whole, *I'm So Free: The 1971 RCA Demos* is not essential, but it is a good, spirited listen to the very foundation of what was to come for the next half-century.

Words and Music, May 1965 (2022)

Our third and final appendix entry takes us the furthest back in time to a post-grad Lou in Freeport, Long Island, New York, in May 1965. The lineage behind these recordings and their subsequent rediscovery is as interesting as the music itself. First, the origins. These songs are all demos, in clear and present folk music form, that Lou recorded with John Cale in the Manhattan apartment Cale shared with Tony Conrad. Lou, living with his parents and doing hack work for Pickwick Records at the time, was 'allowed' to go into the city on weekends, and that's when the two new friends began to cement their creative partnership. This in and of itself is curious, as Cale has stated that his initial meeting with Lou, facilitated by Pickwick's sudden need to create a backing band to put on TV to mime the current Pickwick 'hit' written by Lou – entitled 'The Ostrich' – bore less than encouraging fruit. A quote from Cale on the subject had been made into a wall piece at an exhibition of Lou's papers and belongings at the Lincoln Center New York Public Library for the Performing Arts:

He was trying to get a band together. I didn't want to hear his songs. They seemed sorry for themselves. He'd written 'Heroin' already, and 'I'm Waiting For My Man', but they wouldn't let him record it, they didn't want to do anything with it. I wasn't really interested – most of the music being written then was folk, and he played his songs with an acoustic guitar... They were very different, he was writing about things other people weren't. Their lyrics were very literate, very well expressed, they were tough.

Once Lou and Cale got to know each other creatively, Cale had a change of heart. The songs themselves are all Lou compositions, and feature him on vocals and harmonica (!), with Cale on harmony vocals, but we'll get to the actual music in a bit. This tape was recorded on an at-home reel-to-reel recorder with the intention of Lou using it for songwriter copyright purposes. Once the recordings were completed, Lou took the tape to a local notary in Freeport, and then sealed the tape up in a shipping envelope and popped it in a mailbox to send to himself; this is seen as the 'poor man's copyright', an inexpensive means of securing legal ownership of personally created material. Once Lou had received his package, he kept it, unopened, among his various tools and artifacts, seemingly forgotten about.

Or was it? Fast-forward 50 years, and Don Fleming and Jason Stern had been tasked by Laurie Anderson to clean out and catalog the vast contents of Sister Ray Enterprises, Lou's base of operations for the last decade-plus of his life, before turning over Lou's archives to the New York Public Library of the Performing Arts. The recordings here were found in the same nondescript parcel that Lou had sent to himself, unopened, on a shelf behind Lou's desk and office chair. Timorous with excitement, it took them a period of years to get it together to decide to actually open it. Once preserved and mastered, which, due to the tape's age, required actual white-glove handling, the results saw public release in September 2022.

So, what does it sound like? As stated above, this is, make no mistake, *folk music*, and not simply as a result of the instrumentation. The dour specter of Bob Dylan looms very large here, and while this is generally not surprising, considering the conventions and interests of the era, it is curious with regard to the specific participants. The VU, as well as Lou in particular, took great pains to distinguish themselves from being seen as Dylan-esque also-rans. This may register as little more than youthful competitiveness, but it is worth mentioning the overlapping similarities between the two: the VU was seen as another 'new' act attempting to reach beyond the slim, narrow confines of pop music with the same flavor of 'meaningful' lyrics, featuring tales from the mean streets of NYC, that Dylan had already made a name for himself with. Additionally, the VU was 'led' by a sometimes surly, Jewish, curly-haired singer with a gruff and, at times, tuneless voice. The possible comparisons are not so outlandish as they may seem at first glance. No one was more acutely aware of these concerns than the members of the band; not only were image and surface concerns frequently broadcast as the most important component in any situation in Warhol's Factory, but Dylan himself was known to come around The Factory with his sycophantic entourage, striking up dalliances with both Factory Superstar Edie Sedgwick and Nico, going so far as to give Nico material to sing with the band. This was an unpopular idea. One of the choicest quotes on the whole Dylan/VU nexus comes from Sterling Morrison in Bockris and Malanga's *Uptight*:

> We most certainly did not want to be compared with Bob Dylan or associated with him. We did not want to be near Bob Dylan, either physically or through his songs. When Nico kept insisting that we work up 'I'll Keep it With Mine', for a long time, we simply refused. Then we took a long time to learn it (as long as we could take). After that, even though we knew the song, we insisted that we were unable to play it. We finally did have a go at it on stage, it was performed poorly. We never got any better at it either, for some reason.

This is not only hysterically funny, it is very clear in intention, but what is on this recording is still very early, pre-VU days for Lou's independent songcraft. For someone who had been playing, performing, writing, and even issuing singles while in high school, he had been laboring to produce bland copycat hits for the Pickwick label, but was often given a flat 'no' with regard to the label recording his own compositions. So with his new busking partner, he began at the beginning.

Firstly, there are a few songs here that would see their final public manifestation later on: 'I'm Waiting For the Man' (two versions), 'Heroin', 'Pale Blue Eyes', and the oddity that is 'Wrap Your Troubles in Dreams' that would see an official release of a sort on Nico's first LP, *Chelsea Girl*, followed several decades later with another later-period acoustic demo on the *Peel Slowly And See* box set. Incredibly, there is also a song entitled 'Men of Good Fortune', but the only element it shares with the *Berlin*-era song is its title. The two Banana album classics are generally fully formed here, with a few alterations. The collection starts with the first version of 'I'm Waiting For the Man', and the listener is given their first taste of the music's style and sound quality, which will remain consistent throughout. As to be expected with a recording of this origin and vintage, this is not state-of-the-art, but it is still eminently listenable. The mastering job by John Baldwin and Drew Carroll is exceptional.

Each song is introduced with Lou stating each song's title, followed by 'Words and music, Lou Reed', or some simple variation thereof. This version of the favorite song has a very folksy finger-picked guitar style, while Lou and Cale share an easy, countrified vocal harmony. The most significant aspect of this version is during the 'Hey, white boy' section when it is indeed Cale who responds in a clumsy, gentlemanly tone with 'Oh, not me, Sir...' Both men have an easy comfort with the songs and one another, and this too pervades throughout these recordings. There is frequent quipping and ad-libbing during these recordings. And then there is the harmonica solo. There are in fact, several harmonica solos in these songs, and the truth is that they are perfectly fine. Lou, wearing his 'Dylan harness' that allows him to pick and blow simultaneously, displays a clear affinity for the instrument, despite the sonic comparisons that its presence will undoubtedly create. The additional alternate version is not vastly different, save for an increased tempo and a bizarre on-again, off-again percussion, provided by, presumably, Cale, that resembles coconuts being struck together, or perhaps a spirit-channeling table tapping ritual.

'Heroin', clocking in at a brisk 3:56, starts with Lou fumbling and giggling over his clumsy attempts at authorial declarations. The same country-style guitar picking is here, along with an absence of Cale. The lyrics have a few key changes, the most distinct being the opening line of 'I know just... where I'm going'. While the change in actual syntax is minor, the change in narrative significance is substantial. 'Pale Blue Eyes' features the same chords, but missing are the signifying guitar riffs from the Grey Album, and the lyrics, save for the first stanza, are completely different. Cale does excellent harmony vocals in the chorus. 'Wrap Your Troubles in Dreams' is the track here that has undergone the least amount of editorial change. Cale handles both the vocals and the odd, machine-like percussive strike, while Lou handles the guitar. Like all additional versions, it is overlong at 8:14, but at the same time, of all the songs in this collection, it is the one that points most clearly to the sound of what would come in the future. As stated above, 'Men of Good Fortune' shares nothing beyond the name with the *Berlin* song. What remains is an interesting example of the British street ballad from centuries past. The lyrics speak of a woman lamenting her inevitable spinster status unless a 'man of good fortune' should come courting. It is a fine song, but it is Dylan-esque in the extreme.

What remains is a mixture. Of top interest is the presence of 'Buttercup Song', long thought lost after Sterling Morrison alluded to the early VU rehearsing a version of it. The song itself is remarkable. In waltz time, Lou and Cale open the song by harmonizing the chorus: 'Never get emotionally involved/With man or woman, beast or a child/With cobblestone streets or subway turnstiles/And by World War Three you'll have developed style'. A cautionary street song on love's fickle ways, to be sure. The verses are concerned with various foibles of love and loss, yet it is the performance here that is distinct. Both Lou and Cale create and inhabit showy personas for each character in each verse – the boldness of their delivery verges on musical theater. These two men are clearly having fun with their work and one another. It shows a looseness and humor that became rarer and rarer for each artist as time went on. The other songs betray their influence in both era and style, be they blues or folk numbers, yet all are an interesting listen. The deluxe edition of this release comes with an additional six songs of vintage material from between 1958 and 1964, all under two minutes in length. It's fun listening to early original songs and acoustic guitar exercises, bolstered with a truncated version of Dylan's own 'Don't Think Twice, It's Alright'. It has been stated that there are more archival releases of this sort to come.

Bibliography
Print Media:
Bockris, V., *Transformer: The Lou Reed Story* (Simon and Schuster, 1994)
Bockris, V., Malanga, G., *Uptight: The Velvet Underground Story* (Omnibus Press, 1983)
Cale, J., Bockris, V., *What's Welsh For Zen: The Autobiography Of John Cale* (Bloomsbury, 1999)
Chauncey, G., *Gay New York: Gender, Urban Culture, and the Making of the Gay Male World, 1890-1940* (Basic Books, 1994)
DeCurtis, A., *Lou Reed: A Life* (Back Bay Books, 2017)
Doggett, P., *Lou Reed: Growing Up in Public* (Omnibus Press, 1992)
Kronstad, B., *Perfect Day: An Intimate Portrait of Life With Lou Reed* (Jawbone, 2016)
Larson, S., 'Unboxing Lou Reed's Posthumous Parcel to Himself', *The New Yorker,* 22 September 2022
Levy, A., *Dirty Blvd. The Life and Music of Lou Reed* (Chicago Review Press, 2016)
McKenna, K., *Book of Changes* (Fantagraphics, 2001)
Miles, B., *Zappa: A Biography* (Grove Press, 2004)
Reed, L., *Between Thought and Expression: Selected Lyrics* (Hyperion, 1991)
Reed, L., *I'll Be Your Mirror: The Collected Lyrics* (Hachette Books, 2020)
Reed, L., *My Week Beats Your Year Encounters With Lou Reed*, edited and compiled by Heath, M., and Thomas, P. (Hat and Beard Press, 2018)
Reed, L., *Pass Thru Fire: The Collected Lyrics* (DaCapo, 2008)

Web Resources:
Bradx. 'Lou Reed', *Discogs*, 3 November 2013, https://www.discogs.com/artist/11879-Lou-Reed
'History of National Coming Out Day', *Human Rights Campaign*, 12 October 2008, http://www.hrc/issues/3338.htm
Shepherd, J., 'The Raven', *Lou Reed*, 19 August 2016, https://www.allmusic.com/album/the-raven-mw0000019158/user-reviews
'Lou Reed', *Discogs*, https://www.discogs.com/artist/11879-Lou-Reed
'Lou Reed Discography', *Wikipedia*, 15 November 2022, https://en.wikipedia.org/wiki/Lou_Reed_discography

Film:
The Velvet Underground: A Film by Todd Haynes. Directed By Todd Haynes (Polygram Entertainment, 2021)

Also available from Sonicbond

On Track series
Allman Brothers Band – Andrew Wild 978-1-78952-252-5
Tori Amos – Lisa Torem 978-1-78952-142-9
Aphex Twin – Beau Waddell 978-1-78952-267-9
Asia – Peter Braidis 978-1-78952-099-6
Badfinger – Robert Day-Webb 978-1-878952-176-4
Barclay James Harvest – Keith and Monica Domone 978-1-78952-067-5
Beck – Arthur Lizie 978-1-78952-258-7
The Beatles – Andrew Wild 978-1-78952-009-5
The Beatles Solo 1969-1980 – Andrew Wild 978-1-78952-030-9
Blue Oyster Cult – Jacob Holm-Lupo 978-1-78952-007-1
Blur – Matt Bishop 978-178952-164-1
Marc Bolan and T.Rex – Peter Gallagher 978-1-78952-124-5
Kate Bush – Bill Thomas 978-1-78952-097-2
Camel – Hamish Kuzminski 978-1-78952-040-8
Captain Beefheart – Opher Goodwin 978-1-78952-235-8
Caravan – Andy Boot 978-1-78952-127-6
Cardiacs – Eric Benac 978-1-78952-131-3
Nick Cave and The Bad Seeds – Dominic Sanderson 978-1-78952-240-2
Eric Clapton Solo – Andrew Wild 978-1-78952-141-2
The Clash – Nick Assirati 978-1-78952-077-4
Elvis Costello and The Attractions – Georg Purvis 978-1-78952-129-0
Crosby, Stills and Nash – Andrew Wild 978-1-78952-039-2
Creedence Clearwater Revival – Tony Thompson 978-178952-237-2
The Damned – Morgan Brown 978-1-78952-136-8
Deep Purple and Rainbow 1968-79 – Steve Pilkington 978-1-78952-002-6
Dire Straits – Andrew Wild 978-1-78952-044-6
The Doors – Tony Thompson 978-1-78952-137-5
Dream Theater – Jordan Blum 978-1-78952-050-7
Eagles – John Van der Kiste 978-1-78952-260-0
Earth, Wind and Fire – Bud Wilkins 978-1-78952-272-3
Electric Light Orchestra – Barry Delve 978-1-78952-152-8
Emerson Lake and Palmer – Mike Goode 978-1-78952-000-2
Fairport Convention – Kevan Furbank 978-1-78952-051-4
Peter Gabriel – Graeme Scarfe 978-1-78952-138-2
Genesis – Stuart MacFarlane 978-1-78952-005-7
Gentle Giant – Gary Steel 978-1-78952-058-3
Gong – Kevan Furbank 978-1-78952-082-8
Green Day – William E. Spevack 978-1-78952-261-7
Hall and Oates – Ian Abrahams 978-1-78952-167-2
Hawkwind – Duncan Harris 978-1-78952-052-1
Peter Hammill – Richard Rees Jones 978-1-78952-163-4
Roy Harper – Opher Goodwin 978-1-78952-130-6

Jimi Hendrix – Emma Stott 978-1-78952-175-7
The Hollies – Andrew Darlington 978-1-78952-159-7
Horslips – Richard James 978-1-78952-263-1
The Human League and The Sheffield Scene –
Andrew Darlington 978-1-78952-186-3
The Incredible String Band – Tim Moon 978-1-78952-107-8
Iron Maiden – Steve Pilkington 978-1-78952-061-3
Joe Jackson – Richard James 978-1-78952-189-4
Jefferson Airplane – Richard Butterworth 978-1-78952-143-6
Jethro Tull – Jordan Blum 978-1-78952-016-3
Elton John in the 1970s – Peter Kearns 978-1-78952-034-7
Billy Joel – Lisa Torem 978-1-78952-183-2
Judas Priest – John Tucker 978-1-78952-018-7
Kansas – Kevin Cummings 978-1-78952-057-6
The Kinks – Martin Hutchinson 978-1-78952-172-6
Korn – Matt Karpe 978-1-78952-153-5
Led Zeppelin – Steve Pilkington 978-1-78952-151-1
Level 42 – Matt Philips 978-1-78952-102-3
Little Feat – Georg Purvis - 978-1-78952-168-9
Aimee Mann – Jez Rowden 978-1-78952-036-1
Joni Mitchell – Peter Kearns 978-1-78952-081-1
The Moody Blues – Geoffrey Feakes 978-1-78952-042-2
Motorhead – Duncan Harris 978-1-78952-173-3
Nektar – Scott Meze – 978-1-78952-257-0
New Order – Dennis Remmer – 978-1-78952-249-5
Nightwish – Simon McMurdo – 978-1-78952-270-9
Laura Nyro – Philip Ward 978-1-78952-182-5
Mike Oldfield – Ryan Yard 978-1-78952-060-6
Opeth – Jordan Blum 978-1-78-952-166-5
Pearl Jam – Ben L. Connor 978-1-78952-188-7
Tom Petty – Richard James 978-1-78952-128-3
Pink Floyd – Richard Butterworth 978-1-78952-242-6
The Police – Pete Braidis 978-1-78952-158-0
Porcupine Tree – Nick Holmes 978-1-78952-144-3
Queen – Andrew Wild 978-1-78952-003-3
Radiohead – William Allen 978-1-78952-149-8
Rancid – Paul Matts 989-1-78952-187-0
Renaissance – David Detmer 978-1-78952-062-0
REO Speedwagon – Jim Romag 978-1-78952-262-4
The Rolling Stones 1963-80 – Steve Pilkington 978-1-78952-017-0
The Smiths and Morrissey – Tommy Gunnarsson 978-1-78952-140-5
Spirit – Rev. Keith A. Gordon – 978-1-78952- 248-8
Stackridge – Alan Draper 978-1-78952-232-7

Also available from Sonicbond

Status Quo the Frantic Four Years – Richard James 978-1-78952-160-3
Steely Dan – Jez Rowden 978-1-78952-043-9
Steve Hackett – Geoffrey Feakes 978-1-78952-098-9
Tears For Fears – Paul Clark - 978-178952-238-9
Thin Lizzy – Graeme Stroud 978-1-78952-064-4
Tool – Matt Karpe 978-1-78952-234-1
Toto – Jacob Holm-Lupo 978-1-78952-019-4
U2 – Eoghan Lyng 978-1-78952-078-1
UFO – Richard James 978-1-78952-073-6
Van Der Graaf Generator – Dan Coffey 978-1-78952-031-6
Van Halen – Morgan Brown – 9781-78952-256-3
The Who – Geoffrey Feakes 978-1-78952-076-7
Roy Wood and the Move – James R Turner 978-1-78952-008-8
Yes – Stephen Lambe 978-1-78952-001-9
Frank Zappa 1966 to 1979 – Eric Benac 978-1-78952-033-0
Warren Zevon – Peter Gallagher 978-1-78952-170-2
10CC – Peter Kearns 978-1-78952-054-5

Decades Series

The Bee Gees in the 1960s – Andrew Mon Hughes et al 978-1-78952-148-1
The Bee Gees in the 1970s – Andrew Mon Hughes et al 978-1-78952-179-5
Black Sabbath in the 1970s – Chris Sutton 978-1-78952-171-9
Britpop – Peter Richard Adams and Matt Pooler 978-1-78952-169-6
Phil Collins in the 1980s – Andrew Wild 978-1-78952-185-6
Alice Cooper in the 1970s – Chris Sutton 978-1-78952-104-7
Alice Cooper in the 1980s – Chris Sutton 978-1-78952-259-4
Curved Air in the 1970s – Laura Shenton 978-1-78952-069-9
Donovan in the 1960s – Jeff Fitzgerald 978-1-78952-233-4
Bob Dylan in the 1980s – Don Klees 978-1-78952-157-3
Brian Eno in the 1970s – Gary Parsons 978-1-78952-239-6
Faith No More in the 1990s – Matt Karpe 978-1-78952-250-1
Fleetwood Mac in the 1970s – Andrew Wild 978-1-78952-105-4
Fleetwood Mac in the 1980s – Don Klees 978-178952-254-9
Focus in the 1970s – Stephen Lambe 978-1-78952-079-8
Free and Bad Company in the 1970s – John Van der Kiste 978-1-78952-178-8
Genesis in the 1970s – Bill Thomas 978178952-146-7
George Harrison in the 1970s – Eoghan Lyng 978-1-78952-174-0
Kiss in the 1970s – Peter Gallagher 978-1-78952-246-4
Manfred Mann's Earth Band in the 1970s – John Van der Kiste 978178952-243-3
Marillion in the 1980s – Nathaniel Webb 978-1-78952-065-1
Van Morrison in the 1970s – Peter Childs - 978-1-78952-241-9
Mott the Hoople and Ian Hunter in the 1970s –
John Van der Kiste 978-1-78-952-162-7

Pink Floyd In The 1970s – Georg Purvis 978-1-78952-072-9
Suzi Quatro in the 1970s – Darren Johnson 978-1-78952-236-5
Queen in the 1970s – James Griffiths 978-1-78952-265-5
Roxy Music in the 1970s – Dave Thompson 978-1-78952-180-1
Slade in the 1970s – Darren Johnson 978-1-78952-268-6
Status Quo in the 1980s – Greg Harper 978-1-78952-244-0
Tangerine Dream in the 1970s – Stephen Palmer 978-1-78952-161-0
The Sweet in the 1970s – Darren Johnson 978-1-78952-139-9
Uriah Heep in the 1970s – Steve Pilkington 978-1-78952-103-0
Van der Graaf Generator in the 1970s – Steve Pilkington 978-1-78952-245-7
Rick Wakeman in the 1970s – Geoffrey Feakes 978-1-78952-264-8
Yes in the 1980s – Stephen Lambe with David Watkinson 978-1-78952-125-2

On Screen series
Carry On... – Stephen Lambe 978-1-78952-004-0
David Cronenberg – Patrick Chapman 978-1-78952-071-2
Doctor Who: The David Tennant Years – Jamie Hailstone 978-1-78952-066-8
James Bond – Andrew Wild 978-1-78952-010-1
Monty Python – Steve Pilkington 978-1-78952-047-7
Seinfeld Seasons 1 to 5 – Stephen Lambe 978-1-78952-012-5

Other Books
1967: A Year In Psychedelic Rock 978-1-78952-155-9
1970: A Year In Rock – John Van der Kiste 978-1-78952-147-4
1973: The Golden Year of Progressive Rock 978-1-78952-165-8
Babysitting A Band On The Rocks – G.D. Praetorius 978-1-78952-106-1
Eric Clapton Sessions – Andrew Wild 978-1-78952-177-1
Derek Taylor: For Your Radioactive Children –
Andrew Darlington 978-1-78952-038-5
The Golden Road: The Recording History of The Grateful Dead – John Kilbride 978-1-78952-156-6
Iggy and The Stooges On Stage 1967-1974 – Per Nilsen 978-1-78952-101-6
Jon Anderson and the Warriors – the road to Yes –
David Watkinson 978-1-78952-059-0
Magic: The David Paton Story – David Paton 978-1-78952-266-2
Misty: The Music of Johnny Mathis – Jakob Baekgaard 978-1-78952-247-1
Nu Metal: A Definitive Guide – Matt Karpe 978-1-78952-063-7
Tommy Bolin: In and Out of Deep Purple – Laura Shenton 978-1-78952-070-5
Maximum Darkness – Deke Leonard 978-1-78952-048-4
The Twang Dynasty – Deke Leonard 978-1-78952-049-1

and many more to come!

Would you like to write for Sonicbond Publishing?

At Sonicbond Publishing we are always on the look-out for authors, particularly for our two main series:

On Track. Mixing fact with in depth analysis, the On Track series examines the work of a particular musical artist or group. All genres are considered from easy listening and jazz to 60s soul to 90s pop, via rock and metal.

On Screen. This series looks at the world of film and television. Subjects considered include directors, actors and writers, as well as entire television and film series. As with the On Track series, we balance fact with analysis.

While professional writing experience would, of course, be an advantage the most important qualification is to have real enthusiasm and knowledge of your subject. First-time authors are welcomed, but the ability to write well in English is essential.

Sonicbond Publishing has distribution throughout Europe and North America, and all books are also published in E-book form. Authors will be paid a royalty based on sales of their book.

Further details are available from www.sonicbondpublishing.co.uk. To contact us, complete the contact form there or
email info@sonicbondpublishing.co.uk